RESIST
ENDURE
ESCAPE

Growing Up in Nazi and Communist Hungary

by
Susan F. Darvas

First Person History Series
Summit Crossroads Press
Columbia, Maryland

Publisher: Summit Crossroads Press, Columbia, MD
          Contact: sumcross@aol.com

Library of Congress Control Number:2019909205
ISBN: 978-0-9991565-4-4

Cover Design: SelfPubBookCovers.com/JohnBellArt
Interior Design: Eileen McIntire, eileenmcintire@aol.com

With thanks and appreciation to the United States Holocaust Museum for tpermission to use photos from its archives.

This book is dedicated to my children,
Andrea Darvas Heller and Peter Darvas,
and to my grandchildren,
Lizzie, Tom, Ella, Rachel, and Josef.

Reviewers praise
RESIST, ENDURE, ESCAPE

Dr. Brad Sachs, Ph.D., Psychologist and Best-Selling Author:

Susan Darvas's memoir, *Resist, Endure, Escape*, is a brave and compelling narrative that captures with eloquent prose and bracing, unerring precision a childhood that was circumscribed by the Holocaust. Ms. Darvas's capacity to tell her story reminds us that we are always more than individual particles caught up in historical processes that are at times violent and inhumane, but human beings who ceaselessly seek meaning, relentlessly offer and receive love, and defiantly insist on finding our rightful place in the world. The author has allowed time to knead the tale of what happened to her and transformed her experience into a unique and insightful testament that reminds us that fear and pain, no matter how profound, can never erode the inherent and essential truth that lies at the core of our being.

From BIll Benson, Host of the *First Person* program at the U.S. Holocoaust Memorial Museum:

Resist, Endure, Escape is...intensely personal, revealing, and candid. I closed her memoir not only feeling that I know a great deal more about what Susan went through during the war and the Holocaust, and during the post-war years in Hungary, as it struggled to regain its place in the western world only to be strangled under the "Iron Curtain" of the Soviet Union, but that I know a whole lot more about Susan.

The memoir is intimate. Darvas shares herself throughout, from her fears, hardships, frustrations and pain, to her hopes, dreams, joys, small and large, and her loves, familial and romantic. And while it is intimate and personal, it feels subtle and even understated. But what isn't understated, not because of what Darvas says directly, but infused throughout her journey, is her strength and resilience, traits that have propelled her beyond the bounds of this memoir that ends as she leaves England, and goes on to create and live to this day a remarkable life in the United States.

Of particular significance is the powerful and timely message that Darvas conveys about being an immigrant in a foreign land, reminding us, no, forcing us to understand, that the immigrant experience is universal and so very human, regardless of where the immigrant started their journey.

At its heart, despite the pain, the suffering, the intense sadness in World War II Hungary, Communist Hungary, and struggling to build a life in new foreign lands, it is a story of love. As the memoir opens, "I learned early that being well loved is the most extraordinary gift life can offer." May we all give that gift to another.

Table of Contents

Introduction

Dear Lizzie, Tom, Rachel, Ella, Josef, and Talia,

You often asked me about the past, about growing up during the Holocaust, and afterwards, during the Communist dictatorship. You wanted to know how your grandfather and I escaped from Hungary and how we eventually made it to the United States. You wanted to know how we built a new life out of nothing, what it was like being a refugee. I promised that one day I would tell you all about it.

I am sorry it has taken such a long time to do so. Writing this book turned out to be a major struggle. While I wanted, even needed, to share with you my feelings, thoughts, insights, and experiences magically hidden behind the facade of the everyday and the commonplace, unfortunately there was, and still is, an equally powerful inner drive to avoid writing about my difficult, often traumatic past. Not that it was all dismal, far from it. I was surrounded with much love and joy often enough.

I learned early that being well loved is the most extraordinary gift life can offer. It inoculates against the forces of hate, madness and chaos; it provides a lifeline to survival and wholeness. Love, like a magic wand, illuminates everything in your world. The soul is able to delight in all creation whether it is flooded by the life-giving brilliance of the sun, or by the brooding moon barely illuminating the surrounding darkness. Well, not always. But most of the time anyway…

My parents' love and personal sacrifices provided a protective shield blunting the impact of tragedy and trauma engulfing us during the Holocaust and later the Stalinist regime. Your grandfather's love sustained me during the trials and tribulations of my stormy late teens and early twenties. Our love for each other sustained us in much of our adulthood. Gave us strength to escape the police state of our native land, reinvent ourselves in a different culture on a remote continent, and rebuild our lives laboriously as free citizens in the United States.

Your love and my children's love sustain me in my old age as they have ever since you appeared on this earth. Friendships have sustained me throughout my life. They are a different form of love, equally precious, equally important, perhaps the most selfless in many ways. Love works best when it is reciprocal. When you let it fade, it might fade away completely. Keep that in mind. The only love that never seems to go away is between parents and children. It changes shape perhaps from time to time, but never goes away. And siblings perhaps. I wouldn't know. I am an only child.

You must know that you are well loved by many, including myself, your ancient grandmother. This book is a labor of love first and foremost. It is also a somewhat belated attempt to sort out a lifetime of experiences and challenges and an attempt to pass on lessons learned before I too pass on to parts unknown...

Love,
Your Grandmother Zsuzsi

1. *Goodnight, Anyuka*

It was almost midnight and I was feeling restless. More than restless—out of sorts, exhausted, sluggish, weak, light-headed, sick to my heart. I was in remission from cancer, but that night I began to wonder about the many other ways one can die. Like having a heart attack. There was no reason to believe that I was having a heart attack. Yet something weird was happening.

It all started late in the afternoon after an early dinner with a friend. I was getting ready for a walk in the glowing twilight, but instead I took a nap with the cat on my lap. Unheard of at 7:30 in the evening, after a not particularly taxing day. I slept for almost two hours. Also unheard of. I only woke because Lizzie called. We chatted while she was riding the bus home. Odd, but touching. I still could have walked, I often do around 9:30 or so. I puttered along instead, feeling worse and worse. Nothing hurt, though. I decided to take my blood sugar—maybe that was it? It wasn't, although the first reading was an impossible 64, God knows why. The second try came up with a more convincing 130. Pretty normal for me.

Now it was almost midnight. I had listened to the 11 o'clock news but had no patience with the TV and turned it off after the usual absurdly detailed weather report. Tropical storm/hurricane Bonnie was about to land in North Carolina and most likely bring rain yet again by tomorrow afternoon. Better get some swimming done in the morning before the rain comes. I tried breathing exercises, but for once, this did not make me feel any better. In fact, I was feeling worse. Perhaps a cup of chamomile tea to help settle my insides? I opened the pantry to get the tea. There is a calendar on the pantry door and it said that today was the 27th of May. I knew it was the 27th, but it did not fully register until the date was staring me in the face at close range. May 27th is the date my Mother, Anyu, died, in 1968. Of cancer. That was fifty years ago. The day was almost over and I had not lit her memorial candle. I had not thought of her all day.

I found the candle and lit it. I should have done so the previous night at sunset, according to custom, and it should have burned all day as a reminder of her life and death. I had been preoccupied with my own whims and indulgences and did not have room in my heart for her, just as I hadn't for much of my life. I had cared for her while she was dying, but shut her out while she was living.

As I lit the candle, I felt connected with her for an instant as I tried to conjure up bits and pieces of an ancient prayer. I could picture her lighting the Sabbath candle with a light veil over her dark wavy hair, reciting the blessing. I think it was in Hebrew, but it could have been in Hungarian. I am not sure she understood the Hebrew words she said. But she said them and prayed on the High Holidays. She also had a small, exquisite prayer book with a greenish-silver abalone cover, which contained prayers and poetry in Hungarian, printed in a delicate, cursive script. It is one of the very few things of hers I still have. The poetry was not very good and the prayers were in lofty, supercharged, antiquated Hungarian. We seldom prayed, and I don't pray now. Not formally or predictably. Organized religion is not something I could ever relate to. Sometimes I wish I could. I don't remember Mother lighting candles after the Holocaust. Many people stopped praying after the Holocaust.

Yes, we were Jewish. Sort of. We were what was called at the time "assimilated Jews." Today our family would be described as "cultural or secular Jews." In our case, this meant that we identified mainly as Hungarians and Europeans who also happened to be Jewish. At least that's what we thought.

The tension began to ease from my body as I felt the caress of the tiny flame, and love welled up in my soul, mixed with sadness and sorrow. I poured the tea and began to write at exactly 12:02 am.

I thought Anyuka unpredictable, especially when I was very young. One moment she would be loving, radiating softness and warmth, hugging me close whether I wanted to be hugged or not; the next moment, without visible warning, she would fly into a rage, calling me stupid, nasty, and worse. Hissing like a cat. A feral cat. She never hit me, but I came to be afraid of her and mistrustful. I wanted desperately to figure out what triggered her outbursts, but I couldn't. I thought she was crazy. I know this, because I remember penning a note to myself in desperation to that effect. It was the crude scribble of a four year old. (My father taught me to read and write and my mother drilled me on the multiplication table early on. They must have been bored. I wasn't.) It read something like "Anyu's brain was flushed down the drain." Not a very nice, or accurate, observation. It was the result of utmost frustration, a cry for help. I had no siblings and few friends at the time to talk to, so my lifelong habit of recording feelings of both joy and frustration started early. I remember all this clearly, because all hell broke loose when the note was found. I don't know how it was found. I think Margit, the maid, found it in the wastepaper basket. I also think she thought it was funny. She had that gleam in her eye. In any case, my mother was deeply hurt, angry, and devastated. It did not take much for her to be devastated. She made it clear that I was a nasty, hateful, ungrateful child and that she would never talk to me again. I did

4

Top: My mother Manci.
Below: My father Mano.

not mind that part much—I knew it would not last. Perhaps she was crazy by today's standards. Instability, mood swings, rages, and tantrums tortured her and those of us who were on the receiving end. Father and I were the main recipients.

Father could handle it much better than I could. He was a big man, to begin with. And powerful inside and out. Actually, each of them had a temper, but I could read him better, and his temper was never directed against me. Anyu's whole life was haunted by loss, turmoil, and suffering, some of which I can hardly imagine. She never talked about her mother and sister. They both died young, Grandmother in her mid-forties from peritonitis following gall bladder surgery and my aunt from pneumonia at age sixteen. I never met either of them and I don't remember ever seeing their pictures.

My mother's parents,
Frida & Lipot Herskovics

I have only shadowy memories of my mother's father. A quiet, shy, ineffectual man, always pleasant, etched in various shades of grey. A seemingly empty façade, incapable of affection or family life in a conventional sense. Although he dined with us every Sunday, he never touched and rarely talked to either me or my mother, or anyone else for that matter. He sat quietly, insignificant, melting into the woodwork. He must have had secret qualities hidden from us, as he had married Piroska, a loud, flamboyant, vulgar woman who had a successful business designing and sewing racy outfits for burlesque queens and prostitutes. She had no children of her own and evidently lacked all motherly instincts. There was no love lost between her and my mother. I rarely saw her in my early years, as she apparently was not welcome in our house. I must say that in her brusque way, she was friendly to me on the rare occasions when we encountered each other.

I must have been six or seven when I first saw her workshop, a big room in their apartment in the middle of town, four or five blocks from the "entertainment" district. It was full of old black Singer sewing machines installed inside dark wooden tables. The sewing machines were operated by treading on ornate metal platforms located at the bottom of the tables. There were also rows of tables serving as cutting boards where she designed and laid out her garish garments. There were fabrics in vivid colors and textures, feather boas, clothing scraps, ribbons, beads, and various not-too-subtle adornments. I was fascinated.

Grandfather was supposed to take care of me, but he disappeared after he dropped me off at Piroska's. At first, she was more than happy to show me around, but then she proceeded to ignore me. After watching her for a while, and trying on the bizarre feather and lacy satin concoctions, hats, and shawls, I quickly became bored. The window was open. It was one of those huge 19th or early 20th century windows that start fifteen to twenty inches from the floor and reach almost all the way up to a very high ceiling, with a wide window sill that practically begged to be curled up on, which I did. It was a perfect place to watch the world go by on a very busy street in Pest. We were on the third or fourth floor. There was no screen on the window, nor was there a wrought-iron guard as we were high enough above the street not to have to worry about burglars. It was definitely not a place for anyone to perch, let alone a child. Lean out, perhaps; perch, no.

Piroska did not notice that I was in harm's way, or perhaps she did not care. She was absorbed in her work. I enjoyed my precarious position, fascinated by the spectacle below me. After a while, perhaps ten to fifteen minutes, perhaps more, my inner warning system kicked in. I began to feel light-headed, sensing imminent danger. I got down from the window sill, quickly got bored and probably made a nuisance out of myself. I may have said something at home when asked if I had a good time, because I was never left alone with Piroska again.

In retrospect, this episode is indicative of the parenting, or rather lack of it, Anyu received after her mother's and older sister's premature deaths. It also explains why Anyu was brought up and watched over mostly by my grandmother and her four much-older sons, my uncles. They were all related, as my father's and mother's fathers were first cousins. Are you still with me? In any case, they all watched over her—they practically adopted her. My father was the Chief Adopter. He was the second oldest of the four siblings. The oldest brother, Rezso, was easygoing, jovial, laid back, and pleasant. He knew his mind, but went to great lengths to avoid conflict. I remember that as I grew up and throughout my teens, he would invariably slip me a bank note or two surreptitiously as I was leaving, always making sure to avoid Aunt Jeanette's disapproving vigilance. I was appreciative, but felt uncomfortable.

Rezso was tall and handsome, like all of the brothers except Zoli, the youngest. He had a gift for business, and his customers loved him. I never ever saw him upset or worried. Not even in the midst of disasters. His adoring wife would get extremely frustrated with him when he refused to respond to her passionate complaints about whatever or whomever she was upset about. Jeanette's complaints were many and varied. They were mostly about perceived misdeeds of other people inside and outside the family, and, not infrequently, about me. Jeanette was regarded by the family as a complainer and troublemaker, but nevertheless tolerated for her undeniable business sense, hard work, and devotion to Uncle Rezso. She had been married before, but never had any children as far as I know. I often wondered if that might have had something to do with her joyless disposition.

Emmanuel ("Mano") Leb, my father, was born in Marosvasarhely in the later part of the 19th century in Transylvania, which was then part of Hungary, but is now in Romania. Borders have been shifting forever in that part of the world. In a fit of misguided patriotism, he changed Leb—his original German-Jewish family name—to Lakatos meaning locksmith in Hungarian. I have no idea why he chose this particular name, since he was a dentist and no one in the family had any connection to locks or keys. Choosing to be known by Hungarian names was a rather common practice at the time. Many Jews and others with German sounding names did so in the early years of the twentieth century to show their patriotic fervor.

Markusz, my paternal grandfather I never met.

Paternal grandparents Hannah and Marcusz Leb with my Uncle Zoli in front of their grocery store in Budapest.

Father came from an impoverished branch of an ancient Levite family. Unfortunately, I know next to nothing about them. I recall hearing that his father made a living traveling with a horse-drawn buggy to remote parts of Transylvania, selling pots and pans and other necessities to the villagers. He lived long enough to sire four sons, but died at a young age from some sort of sepsis. Information about him is scarce. I never met him. It was left to my grandmother to bring up her sons, which she did successfully, although not without a great deal of hardship. Her name was Hannah. She only finished fourth grade, but still managed to transform a vegetable stand into a small grocery store and made sure that her sons received high school diplomas, or more in my father's case. Father became a highly successful professional, read and traveled widely, and provided my mother and myself with a comfortable middle-class life as long as he could, which was not very long, as history intervened.

As my grandmother grew older, Father assumed the family leadership, though Grandmother nominally retained her matriarchal status. In addition to being politically and professionally influential, Father apparently was a man about town, charismatic, a magnet for women. His girlfriends were numerous and spectacular. He also traveled widely for the times. His enthusiasm for the richness of life and adventure were contagious. When I was sitting on his lap, hardly more than a toddler, he showed me a map of the world. Instead of reading me fairy tales, he taught me the names of the continents and described the wonders and secrets they

Three generations of women: my paternal grandmother and my mother, eight months pregnant with me.

held in fragrant words. Thank you, Apu, for unlocking my mind and heart to adventure and so much more.

As the story goes, it was not until Father hit forty that he discovered that his fun but troublesome pet, my future mother, his niece once removed, was actually a full-grown woman. A beautiful, energetic, loving creature who adored him. And only him. She was fond of all of her uncles, but loved only him. She was not sophisticated like his girlfriends, or self-sufficient, nor did she have money, but she needed him for protection and guidance. Or so he thought, and apparently so my mother thought. Actually, I don't really know what my mother thought. I heard the story from my father and my uncles. My mother never talked about it or anything else about her life before she got married. As though it did not exist. As though her life began and ended with my father. She survived him by less than two years. And she was not quite fifty-eight when she died. He was eighteen years older.

Anyway, they got married. And I was born eight months later. I never questioned this until well into adulthood. Then I shrugged and abandoned further inquiry. Was I premature, or did my fetus presence force my father's hand to marry? Perhaps, but then what? They were destined for each other, lifelong partners in a dedicated, symbiotic, if stormy, relationship. My role, apparently from inception, was to mediate between them, to be the visible link, the easer of tensions, the voice of reason. It didn't always work, and it may just have been my fantasy. In any case, real or imagined, the role gave me some illusion of control and a reason for being proactive rather than just hiding under the bed. For it was frightening, very frightening, when they fought, and they fought frequently.

Was anyone surprised by the marriage? I don't know. Disappointed? Perhaps. At any rate, my mother never quite felt accepted by her much-older sisters-in-law. She was the junior kid on the block—she did not fit in. She was not only much younger, but her transformation from family pet to equal status did not go smoothly. She did not fit the mold of the respectable matron. She was young, pretty, spontaneous, and artistic. She did not know how to hide her feelings. She was outspoken. Diplomatic skills eluded her. She did not play by the rules. Also, though she did not know it, she was brighter than my aunts, better read, and more creative, with a highly developed aesthetic sense. By the time I was old enough to remember, she had become an inspired cook and baker. She created intricate lace tablecloths and knit exquisite dresses and suits for me and for herself. I still have one of her tablecloths made of delicate, paperthin, ecru yarn in an intricate mandala design.

My mother's hands were always perfectly manicured and never disfigured by manual work. Nothing more taxing than crocheting delicate tablecloths or knitting beautiful dresses were required of those hands. Cooking and baking meant mostly supervising. Even when she cooked, she had a sous-chef in Margit, the live-in house-keeper, maid, cleaning woman, and child-minder. We lived a life of middle-class privilege which included Margit and a washer woman once a month for big stuff, such as bed linen, towels, tablecloths, etc. There was also a wash day every week for everyday stuff. I liked our washerwoman especially since she usually allowed me to help, and we worked side by side when Mother was not around. Mother did not approve of my fraternizing with the HELP. Poor mother, there came a time when she had to do all of the above by herself and would have been grateful for any help at all. In any case I was allowed to wash small things like panties, socks, and handkerchiefs in the sink or in the wooden washtub. I was very proud of this. There was also an ironing day, and once a month a mending and sewing day. Seasonal and minor alterations, changing hems, mending socks and other chores were performed by a seamstress on our foot-pedaled Singer sewing machine. The seamstress was not trusted with new clothing though. That was custom made by a downtown salon or tailors. So were our shoes. I loved those shoes.

Mother had her limits, of course. She hated Picasso and abstract art and thought Freud was a crank. But at least she knew they exist-ed. With no formal education beyond high school, she read broadly and voraciously. For someone as insecure as she was, she had strong, often misguided, opinions about everything under the sun. The rest of the family, except for my father, had little interest in broader intel-lectual pursuits and the arts. They had the ubiquitous, depressingly dark landscape paintings on their busily wallpapered walls, alongside the inevitable faded family photographs. There were porcelain figurines, mostly hand-painted Herendi, entrapped in bulky display cabinets. Dainty, colorful birds, ever-smiling shepherds and shepherdesses with blank faces, goose herders in native costumes with their geese, pill boxes, glittering crystal wine glasses, burgundy-and-blue Austrian crystal vases with silver rims—objects of busy beauty brightening humdrum middle-class lives. Distractions from tragedy and despair crouching expectantly just around the corner.

My youngest aunt, Juci, was even less accepted than my mother. She was from Szabadka, then still part of imperial Hungary. She was a single mother with a teenage son. Perhaps once married, perhaps not, which was not an asset in 1930s Hungary or anywhere else in Europe. Juci was extraordinarily beautiful and blessed with a sweet, caring nature. Zoli was enchanted by her, much to the disapproval of the family, especially my grandmother. (Oh, my grandmother! But that is another story.) To keep the peace, Zoli did not marry Juci for a long time. He supported her and Pista, her son, but did not marry her until Pista died. He shot himself, around age nineteen, supposedly by accident, but more likely to pave his mother's way to marriage, or so the story goes. Pista thought that he was a barrier to his mother's happiness and security. Apparently, this was not true. He was bright, handsome and kind, well-liked by all. In any case there were other considerable barriers to a Zoli-Juci marriage. For one thing, Juci was—and remained—a Catholic. Zoli thought it would be dangerous for her to marry

Zoli and Juci's wedding

a Jew. Nevertheless, they were married after Pista's death.

My father was what I would now call an agnostic—a Jewish agnostic. Garrison Keillor's description of a resident of Lake Wobegon comes to mind: "He was an atheist, but a Lutheran atheist. He disbelieved in a Lutheran God." My father disbelieved in a Jewish God. He made me aware and proud of the fact that instead of 2000 years, we had a history of more than 5000 years. We had distinguished ancestors who had shaped Western culture. We were the People of the Book. We thought we had invented monotheism. Maybe we did. All this helped me to appreciate my heritage without being bound by it. It helped me reject the systematic process of destroying self-esteem and self-confidence practiced by the Nazis, who were masters of denigration and pronounced us inferior. All racists do this. They share the same script.

Father was a humanist. His spirit embraced the whole world and everything in it. Like Bertrand Russell, he mistrusted organized religion. He also mistrusted Marx, Lenin, Stalin, and rigid ideologies. He thought the Old Testament was a collection of fascinating stories, like Greek mythology, or Grimms' and Andersen's fairy tales, or Charles Lamb's retelling of Shakespeare's plays. He made sure I was familiar with all of them at a tender age.

To my father, religion was not much different from fairy tales. He had a fierce spirit, a warrior's spirit, and his moral code was impeccable. He was proud of being a Hungarian—proud of the culture and the literary and artistic accomplishments of a small nation that had been engaged in a constant struggle over millennia to maintain its freedom and identity. In that respect, Hungarians were very much like Jews, except there was a country called Hungary. Truncated, but still there. Israel was dreamt of by only a few at that time, as far as we knew.

Father avoided synagogues or any other forms of worship. Still, both he and mother, and later, I myself fasted on Yom Kippur, and I remember celebrating High Holidays at the home of distant relatives we never saw otherwise. I was taught to recite the "Manishtana" because I was always the youngest one and often the only child. I pretty much disliked doing it, since even then I had trouble praising God for the indiscriminate extinction of Egyptian civilians by plague, etc. I was particularly appalled by the killing of firstborns, evidently a favored practice in the ancient Middle East. After all, I was a firstborn. A girl, granted, but a firstborn. Anyway, I remember being happy enough to search for the afikomen, a piece of matzoh hidden somewhere not too difficult to find. If you found it, you were given a small present. Nothing terribly exciting—it was the search that was fun after the interminable Seder. This was pretty much the extent of my early Jewish identity. I did learn to value, celebrate, and be passionate about freedom and to be willing to take risks to achieve and maintain it. Perhaps these memories worked obscurely in the background much later when I made the decision to escape from Hungary, my modern-day Egypt, to freedom. We left no plague behind, except that created by a vicious regime for itself.

The family gave equal time to Christianity. Christmas and Easter were celebrated at Juci and Zoli's house. I loved those holidays. I loved the sweet fondants Juci baked and wrapped in tin foil and tissue paper fringed at both ends. They were orange-, lemon-, strawberry-, mocha-, and chocolate-flavored. I loved the chocolate and mocha ones best. I also loved the beautiful live Douglas fir reaching high toward the ceiling, decorated lovingly with great skill by Juci and with considerably less skill by me. I loved the tiny flickering candles clipped to the branches in their tin holders, throwing ever-shifting shadows when lit after dark. They were probably a fire hazard, but no one seemed to worry. The candles illuminated and added sparkle to all the gilded decorations, hiding their tawdriness and suggesting mystery and magic. The magic of peace and love and light. Of giving. Of hope in renewal and rebirth. Once again, we chose to ignore the inevitable seamy side of the message. Love and Birth followed by Persecution. Crucifixion. Martyrdom. We ignored it for we must have sensed that it was waiting for us in reality.

There were always wonderful gifts under the tree for all of us. I remember clearly the red bicycle I dreamt about for so long. Until then all I had was a tricycle. Tricycles were for babies. It was an embarrassment. I also remember a pair of skis years later. I don't think I ever used them. Even as an adult, I never developed a taste for skiing. Too cold, too wet. I liked sledding, though. It was less risky. When you fell, you did not fall far. Most of the gifts were welcome, anticipated, and wonderful. So was Christmas dinner. Juci was a wonderful cook. We always had roast stuffed goose. Hungarians didn't eat turkeys. They exported them, but refused to eat them. The meat was considered too bland, too dull. There was roast suckling pig for New Year's and lamb for Easter. And pastries. The cakes and cookies were a spiritual experience. Really.

The most wonderful experience for me was Midnight Mass. Only Juci and I went. We took the bus to ancient Var Castle in Buda. The Mass was held in the Matyas Cathedral, an exquisite nine-hundred-year-old gothic structure that had not yet been destroyed by war. My spirit took wings there, exploring the upward curves of the amazing structure and savoring the beauty of the illuminated stained glass embracing us from all sides and from above, extending the horizon to what seemed like infinity. The music and light and magical space worked together to awaken my spirit and inspired me to reach for the unreachable, for the eternal. I loved Midnight Mass. I loved being with Juci. We did not ever have much to say to each other, but she knew how to love; she understood. We played together, we laughed together, we loved animals together, and we loved each other. She was my favorite aunt.

You have gathered by now that Juci was beautiful, inside and out. She had warm, cornflower-blue eyes radiating love and naturally wavy honey-colored hair framing a heart-shaped face. Her mouth was designed for caring words and possibly for making love. I never heard her raise her voice. She was fiercely protective when it came to Zoli and us and animals of all kinds. She stood by us all through the persecutions and brought much-needed food to the ghetto at considerable personal danger and sacrifice. She sheltered Zoli for as long as she could, but eventually he was forced to join us in the ghetto after he was betrayed by informants. Juci was relatively safe, but she was shunned by most of the neighbors because she was married to a Jew and refused to divorce him.

She had other problems as well. Pets were not allowed in the apartments, so she decided to feed the pigeons instead. Some neighbors strongly disapproved. There were reasons for this. She transformed the building into Saint Mark's Square at feeding times, twice a day. The pigeons filled the courtyard, perching on the wrought-iron guardrails, fluttering around frantically, and greedily gobbling the bread crumbs and other edibles Juci provided for them. They chattered excitedly, fought over the food, and left behind, as pigeons do, droppings, feathers, and other debris. The children in the house loved it, but the neighbors were not amused. Neither were the Hazmesters. This became a big problem.

The Hazmesters (or concierges) were all-powerful in apartment buildings in Hungarian cities. They were usually a hardworking couple with little education. They kept the building, if not sparkling clean, at least habitable and did small repairs in exchange for a small apartment, a meager salary, and the obligatory tips from tenants. The upkeep of those old buildings was hard work indeed and they were on call 24/7. They were the Guardians of the Gates, who controlled access to the building by opening and shutting the heavy front gate in the morning and evening. These were very heavy wood and metal doors, reminiscent of medieval fortresses. To get in after hours, you had to ring the Hazmesters, and they "opened sesame" for you. They were privy to everyone's comings and goings even during the day, because their apartment had a window opening to the entrance of the building. They cleaned the courtyard and the gangways (folyoso) that surrounded it on four sides. Typically, these older city buildings were built around a rectangular inner courtyard. The large apartments ran the depth of the building and had entrances on the tiled gangways surrounding them. The gangways had pretty wrought-iron railings to protect against fatal falls.

The Hazmesters hated the pigeons and a war between them and my sweet and mild aunt became inevitable. There was much shouting, cursing, and threatening from below. Juci said nothing; she was not the shouting, cursing kind. She just kept on feeding the pigeons. It was not an altogether wise move. The Hazmesters often supplemented their meager income not only with tips from residents, but also by tipping off law enforcement. During the Nazi Regime, that meant lawlessness enforcement. They often became informants. On the other hand, they sometimes became rescuers by withholding information on a hidden Jew or Resistance fighter. In any case, Juci had to stop feeding the pigeons in order to protect herself and keep Zoli safe.

She resumed Operation Pigeon when the war ended in Budapest in the spring of 1945.

2. The Ark

I have always thought that there must have been warnings that No- ah heeded, but others did not. Perhaps there was a gradual climate change. Did a Biblical global warming, with frequent storms and unusual weather patterns, make Noah decide to build an ark? He must have thought there was nowhere to go on land. Nowhere that was safe. Besides, he heard voices. The voice of God! In those days this was not considered psychotic. Weird perhaps, and people were laughing, but Noah did not care, at least not enough to abandon his project. He stubbornly followed his intuition, as we would call it today. He stopped cultivating his land, or tending his sheep, or what- ever he was supposed to do, and devoted his days to constructing the ark to prepare an escape route. For himself, his family, and the creatures who were willing to join him. His fellow humans, despite his urging, did not bother to build their arks. They were not willing to abandon their accustomed and reasonably comfortable life, their possessions, such as they were, and their belief that things could not get much worse. They did not believe that the unimaginable could happen, or that it could happen to them. Noah completed his ark, loaded up his family and the creatures, and sailed away safely when the flood came, as he knew it would. He left most of his possessions behind, but he survived.

My father was definitely not a modern-day Noah, in spite of being a visionary. He foresaw many of the scientific "miracles" to come in the 20th and 21st centuries, but he could not envision Apocalypse. It was not in his nature. Even as the signs mounted, even after Kristallnacht and the annexation of Austria, even after Hitler took full control of Germany and all the news media paraded his military might and murderous hatred of Jews and his contempt of all non-Aryans, even after Jews were barred from most schools and pro-fessions, beaten up and persecuted, even after legislation limited the number of Jewish students who could attend university in Hungary, or enter professions, Father still did not see the fast approach of Di-saster. He could not believe that insanity would take hold of civilized Germany and semi-civilized Hungary. He stayed put, and so did my uncles, and so did most of the Hungarian Jews. They stayed and were engulfed by the Nazi Flood. There were around eight hundred thousand Jews in Hungary in 1944. Within a year, at the end of the War, five hundred sixty-five thousand were murdered.

Uncle Laci was our Noah, the only one of my father's three brothers who had the foresight and courage to leave, to sail away to England and start a new life in the nick of time. Literally. In 1939, just a couple of weeks before WWII officially began. I have always admired him for that, in spite of the fact that in the end he did not survive, at least not for very long. His two children, my only cousins, Magdi, then twelve, and Imre, five, did live, but paid a heavy price. In some ways they had perhaps an even rougher time in England, supposedly out of harm's way, than I did stranded in the middle of the Holocaust. It appears that arks can sink too and the Gods of yore are still up to their cruel and capricious tricks.

Consider this: Laci died alone, in a hotel, on a business trip, os-tensibly from a defective, leaking shilling-fed gas heater, sometime in 1945. Just months after the war ended. Or perhaps just as the war was ending. He was found in the morning, sitting in a chair with the daily paper in his hands. He was effectively gassed in his very own

My father, Uncle Rezso, and Uncle Laszlo (Laci)

private gas chamber in a small hotel in Manchester, England. His two children were orphaned. Magdi, then around sixteen, had lost her mother soon after she was born. Imre, then around ten, had his mother after a fashion, but she was very ill and wheelchair bound with multiple sclerosis or something similar. This was beyond irony. It struck me even then as a mysterious malevolent cosmic joke.

In 1939, I was not in any position to leave, since I was only five years old. By 1940 it was too late. We were trapped in Hungary. Father thought our best bet was to try to stay one step ahead of the Nazis and avoid being deported to a concentration camp. There were no concentration camps yet in 1939, and when there were, we didn't hear about them at first. When we finally did, my parents and most Jews refused to believe they existed. I heard later that when Mengele separated the wheat from the chaff in Auschwitz—that is the able-bodied who could work from the children and the infirm who were destined to be murdered—most of them marched unquestioningly to the "showers," never to be seen again in human form. They went up in smoke, close to six million of them. Their molecules entered the atmosphere before joining the vastness of a non-discriminating Universe. These "Jewish" molecules became part of the Nazis' atmosphere, the air they inhaled and the air they exhaled. They entered the bodies of their Nazi persecutors, their fields and gardens, their livestock. Their tortured molecules then moved over the continent and over the oceans to other continents until the whole world became saturated by the physical components of the murdered Jews.

One Sunday when I was six or so, we had unusual guests at the dinner table. I had never seen them before. They were unlike us, although they were evidently distant relatives on my father's side from Erdely or Transylvania (now in Romania). They were Orthodox Jews with sideburns and beards, more comfortable with Yiddish than with Hungarian. They were strangely dressed. They spoke with an accent. They spoke of persecutions and pogroms and deportations. Famine. I only understood them sporadically. They seemed overwhelmed by the glamour of the beautiful table in our bright sunny dining room, which was set with a spotless carefully ironed lace tablecloth and our good china, and laid with an abundance of food. Freshly baked bread, chicken soup with delicious light dumplings, freshly slaughtered chicken deep fried to a delicious crispy crunch, hand-sliced paper-thin flash-fried potato chips (Roscheibni), cucumber salad, and vegetables. For dessert there was the usual feather-light cake filled with chocolate/mocha buttercream filling (Piskotatorta) accompa

Me, unaware of the storm to come.

nied by freshly whipped cream and espresso coffee.

We were still in heaven, but the visitors were the Messengers of Doom! Literally. They spoke in hushed tones of how they had to escape in the middle of the night, leaving everything behind. How their friends and relatives were deported and taken to concentration camps where unimaginable horrors awaited them. How they thought they could find shelter in Hungary, but now that they were here, they knew they had to leave again. I only caught bits and pieces of their narrative, and I did not understand much of it at the time. Still, suddenly the light went out for me. The sun vanished and the wings of fear and horror enveloped me. I could not understand how everyone could go on eating peacefully, smiling, chewing, and chatting as though nothing had happened. I could not. I had to leave the table; otherwise I would have thrown up. Later that day I was told I was silly. It could never happen to us. But I knew better. Don't ask me how, but I knew. The Age of Innocence was over.

3. *Sparrows, Pigeons and Metaphors*

I loved the outdoors and non-competitive solitary physical activities when I was young. I rode my bike every day, exploring the steep hills with glee and exulted in the freedom of flying downhill after the strenuous long rides up. I can still feel the intense pleasure of the wind rushing by me and the challenge of staying upright on the rough road. Naturally, I crashed often. I still have bits of charcoal and other debris embedded in my right knee after a particularly nasty fall on Pagony ucca, a very steep unpaved road. I was known in the neighborhood for my assorted scars and perpetually bandaged knees. It is a miracle I never had a concussion (as far as I know). I had neither helmet nor jeans and rode without padding of any sort. I also spent long hours on foot wandering the surrounding Buda hills, absorbing the strength, the beauty, and the accepting embrace of the landscape. I came to know each hill, the trails in the forest, and the assorted creatures going about their business. I never felt lonely outdoors. I still don't.

I loved to watch and listen to the birds around the house. Sparrows, pigeons, and robins went about their business, like accountants or school children doing their chores, but the swallows were special, grace personified. They were absurdly beautiful, living in some sort of accelerated universe, their rapid non-linear movements orchestrated to a rhythm I could neither hear nor fathom.

I loved them all, but I deeply mistrusted sparrows at an early age. They stole things. Whenever an annoying or dangerous toy or another prized possession went missing, Mother and Margit insisted that the sparrows had taken it. Not the bogey man, but sparrows. And there they were, every morning when I woke up, outside my window, chattering on the trees, spying on me, plotting what to steal next. No, I was not paranoid, just a very gullible four-to-six-year-old with too much imagination for her own good. And very trusting, except for the sparrows of course.

Actually, there was a problem with the pigeons, too. They were so very elusive. They would swoop in and settle tantalizingly close, doing away greedily with whatever crumbs they could find and begging for more. They allowed me to watch their squabbles, the mini-dramas of competing for food. I gave names to the regulars. There was Baldy, who was often bullied; Lucille, a very pretty, slender adolescent with silvery gray feathers; Harvey, the bully, shoving everyone aside; Snow White, radiant and graceful; and Speedy, who swooshed in and out so rapidly that by the time the others realized he was stealing their best morsels, he was gone. I saved pieces of bread from the table and got more from the kitchen and raced outside after dinner to feed them. They gathered close around me. I felt like a Queen dispensing largesse to my subjects. I felt trusted and loved, until I ran out of food. Then they all left, and I was alone once again. It was a letdown, a disappointment, a betrayal. I wanted to express my love not just through food, but by picking them up, stroking them, and keeping them around. They would not let me.

I asked Margit for advice. She grabbed a handful of salt from the salt cellar in the kitchen. "Select your favorite pigeon and sprinkle the salt on its tail feathers," she said. "It doesn't have to be your favorite. It will work on any pigeon," she added after due consideration.

My mother confirmed this when I consulted her on the matter.

From then on, I spent many hours raiding the salt cellar and chasing pigeons. Frustrating as it was, I rather enjoyed this. It became a game. The pigeons were clever. They led me on. They would flee a short distance, then settle down again tantalizingly close but always just out of reach. I admired them for their precision, persistence, and willingness to court danger in order to get something they wanted. The sparrows were different; they flew away, chattering contemptuously, and vanished completely whenever I tried to make friends or told them to stop taking my things.

"I get close, but never close enough to put the salt on their tail," I complained to Margit in tears.

"You have to try harder. Sneak up on them. Try again and again!"

I did, until the futility of it all dawned on me.

"It is not possible. If I could get close enough to salt them, I would be close enough to catch them," I finally said.

This great insight was greeted with laughter. Not exactly unkind, just amused with a hint of "we got ya!"

I was not amused.

Birds were great teachers. The pigeons and sparrows taught me a lot about people. I made it a rule, at a tender age, not to follow instructions blindly. I had to make sure they made sense. Observing this rule often got me in trouble later, but it also helped me stay alive. The pigeon adventure also taught me that people I trusted and loved could lie for

Me, feeling quite grown-up on my first tricycle

many reasons, even merely for their own amusement. The difference between jokes and lies can be rather subtle...

My parents decided that it was time for me to enter first grade when I was not quite five. I remember talking to friendly strangers, answering questions, solving problems. It did not occur to me that I was being "tested." I have only vague memories now, except that I rather enjoyed most of it. I remember two things in particular. I was presented with some sort of mechanical puzzle: small metal bricks and gears piled on top of each other with random spaces in between. The pieces were held together by a rod in the center and a screw on top. I certainly had never seen anything like that before. I was told to move one of the bricks to the top.

"Take your time, and I'll come back later to see how you are doing," said the nice woman, who then left me alone in the room.

I looked at the thing and began to experiment by moving around the pieces that were moveable. I had zero mechanical interest or aptitude then, and not much more now. I have never liked puzzles. After a few minutes, I lost interest and started looking for a more efficient solution. I unscrewed the top, disassembled the mechanism to remove the targeted metal piece, and inserted it where it was supposed to be moved. I screwed the top back in place and relaxed. The nice lady came back, ready to help. When I told her all was well and showed her the puzzle, she was stunned.

"You didn't have enough time. How did you do it?"

"I just took the top off and then it was really easy," I told her.

"That was not what you were supposed to do," she said, shaking her head. "But you solved the puzzle. You don't have to do it again."

The other test I remember was a pattern of dots that I was supposed to connect to create a pattern. I produced a series of laughing carrots for some obscure reason. I thought they were funny, and they did produce general merriment and consternation.

I am pretty sure they thought I was insane, but they placed me in first grade anyway. This was a mixed blessing. I did not have trouble with the academics but I was a full year-and-a-half younger than my schoolmates and had limited social skills. Being an only child gave me little experience with other kids. I had hung around adults all my life up to this point. This created problems, but I learned fast. All in all, I rather enjoyed the English-Hungarian Embassy School. It was not exactly bilingual, but we were taught conversational English every day. Seventy-five years later, I am still in touch with a couple of my schoolmates.

This brief period of bliss did not last long. The English-Hungarian School was shut down after diplomatic relations with Britain were terminated in 1939. For me that meant no more elite school with gifted and privileged students, no more bilingual instruction or enlightened curriculum. I was transferred to a local public elementary school where the biggest challenges were coloring within the prescribed lines, learning how to knit, and listening to other kids call me a "Dirty Jew."

I was puzzled. These kids were my neighbors; they knew us. Why did they suddenly mind that my parents were Jewish, that I was Jewish? I was not religious anyway. I did not mind what their religion was. Catholic or Protestant, I could not care less. I spoke and wrote better Hungarian than most of my classmates, so why was I considered evil and inferior, and despised? I was confused and angry, and I wanted to understand. I tried to open up a dialogue, a discussion to put things right. Really! I was that naïve; after all, I was still not much more than six years old and in first grade again. There was no accelerated education for a Jew anymore and pretty soon, there was no education for a Jew at all. The phrase "ethnic cleansing" did not exist yet, but it was about to happen. In fact, it was already in progress. I did not know this. I just felt bewildered, frightened, and incredulous.

I thought they were all mad, but this did not prevent the slow erosion of my self-confidence. The image of myself as caring, giving, and gifted, a worthy and loving child, was challenged with relentless regularity until I began to wonder if they were right. That's what abuse and persecution do to you. They attack not only your body, but also aim at destroying your soul. Even then, I knew that I couldn't—wouldn't— allow that to happen to me.

In school, we were taught that the Allies were evil and the Nazis pure and virtuous knights in shining armor. They would win the war and rule the world. I did not believe this, but I knew that I must not say so. Everything seemed strange, hostile and unreal. I was alternately harassed and avoided. I was now an outcast. I had no idea how to deal with this.

Cognitive dissonance entered my life. For example, we were instructed to knit scarves and socks in class for the soldiers fighting on the Eastern Front in the unforgiving Russian winter. I certainly did not want the Hungarian soldiers to win the war. It would mean that the Nazis prevailed and my family and I would die. But I did not want the fathers and brothers of my classmates and friends to freeze to death either. So, I continued to knit scarves and socks, feeling confused and conflicted. I hoped the Nazis would not win because of my scarves and socks. Just in case, I made sure that they were not very nice scarves and socks. Actually, come to think of it, I never learned to be a really good knitter.

Around 1942 or 1943, the Allied bombings began. Initially, only factories, railroads, and other strategic destinations in and around Pest were targeted. In Buda, we seemed far removed and my father considered us safe, at least from the bombs. My mother disagreed. I took my cue from Father, as usual. I remember when I first began to have my doubts. It was a beautiful, sunny, peaceful summer day and I was climbing a cherry tree in the garden. Father waved to me from the upstairs balcony.

"Come quick! I want to show you something."

He seemed excited. It took me a few seconds to get down from the tree, munching the cherries I had just picked. I rushed upstairs. He pointed at the sky in the distance, across the river, beyond the city. I could see tiny objects no bigger than gnats buzzing around. They were bombers and fighter planes; you could not tell them apart from this distance. Random flashes of light exploded around the planes and beneath them on the ground. At times, one of the planes would take a direct hit and fall rapidly like a shooting star. There was no way of telling how the battle was going, who was who, or which was which. It was spectacular; it was awesome, like in the movies. Except it was real. I had never seen anything like it.

"We are safe here in Buda," Father reassured me. "The British are here. They are destroying the airfields, the war machine. They won't harm civilians. They will drive the Germans out and we will all be free and safe again…"

Father believed this with all his heart. He was off on a few crucial counts, such as timing, and he had an inordinately optimistic view of our chances of survival, among other things. I could see puffs of smoke forming wispy clouds around planes, then flashes of blood-red lights as aircraft were hit and fell out of the sky, one after another. I saw fires burning in the distance where the bombs had fallen. It did not seem all that safe to me. And I didn't see how father could tell if the right planes were being shot down. Everything was distant and had an unreal quality. My muscles tensed and my chest and stomach became tight. Mother wanted me to come inside. She was clearly frightened.

A few months later, the air raid sirens began to sound in the hills of Buda as well. I could not imagine what the targets were. Did our rescuers think that the birds and the bees, the squirrels and the trees were aiding the Nazis? Did they not worry about hitting us, who were on their side? My child's brain could not understand what was happening. I still cannot comprehend mass destruction as a legitimate technique of war, for whatever reason. The seeds of wariness of not only enemies, but also of powerful friends, were planted early, only to be reinforced by our "liberation" by the Soviet Army a couple of years later.

My mother was way ahead of me in this regard. She hid in the narrow, dark cellar that served as our pantry. The shelves on both sides of the walls were filled with a multitude of jars of sour cherries, apricots, plums, raspberry jam, and vegetables canned over the summer and glowing like jewels in the dim light. There were sacks of flour and sugar, and precious ounces of tea leaves and coffee beans. Smoked hams, salamis, and smoked sausages in pairs hung from the ceiling and seemed to sway in the flickering light, until the electricity went out and we had only the faint hovering light of a single candle to illuminate the gloomy darkness. Power outages were becoming increasingly frequent and candles were in short supply. Flashlights had to be used sparingly as batteries were extremely scarce. We had a special flashlight powered by rapidly cranking a lever. It was hard work for very feeble and short-lived light. We also had water stored in the cellar for drinking and for putting out fires should a bomb fall. Even if the house collapsed above us, we would not to starve for a while.

Mother spent a lot of time in that cold, damp cellar, huddled on a small stool wrapped in blankets and demanding that I do the same to stay safe. I could not bear it for very long. My mother's fear filled the small narrow space and I had to escape the dark wings of her anxiety, before I too was engulfed in it. So I stayed with my father upstairs, watching the aerial fireworks, visiting her only for brief periods and when the bombs started falling closer. After the all-clear, we went upstairs again to check for stray fires and survey the damage.

In retrospect, ours was still a relatively safe and serene existence in view of what was soon to come. We had our home, food, and water. True, we had to put up with increased threats and harassment, but my father could still work some and we were able to come and go more or less as we pleased. Most importantly, we had each other. It was not to last.

Soon I was not allowed to go to school anywhere at all. I was not allowed to roam the neighborhood or to leave the house by myself. It was too dangerous. Although nobody told me exactly what might happen, I knew that my parents were worried and I must stay in. This turned out not to be too difficult. Former schoolmates avoided me or pretended not to know me. The more honest or naïve confided, "I am not allowed to play with you anymore, because you are a dirty, stinky Jew." They would glance around making sure that anyone who was watching would not think they were fraternizing with a Jew.

There were informants everywhere, my father explained. A yellow brick apartment building, about five stories high, that dominated the surrounding landscape was appropriated by Nazi officials and their families. The German House, as it was called, sported the Nazi flag. They did not want their children to be around Jewish children and they did not want to be contaminated by Jewish presence themselves. I had no idea how they knew who was Jewish and who was not. There weren't many Jews in the neighborhood. It became clear that we were considered not only unclean, but downright dirty, contaminating the very air they breathed, like toxic bacteria. I knew this from the newspapers, the radio broadcasts, and the personal remarks of total strangers. I am not making this up! Epithets like "Dirty Jew" were commonplace, dropped like bricks by passing neighbors and their teenagers. They were printed on posters and flyers along with distorted, predatory, barely human faces with huge hooked noses and skeletal fingers grasping banknotes and gold, dripping blood for good measure. I am not exaggerating. Look it up in history books.

I was disturbed, but mostly puzzled. I definitely did not smell. My mother insisted that I wash thoroughly with soap and warm water every day, even when she could not use the bathtub anymore and had to heat the water on the stove. She poured the warm water into a large enameled basin and set it on the table in the kitchen. It was a painstaking process; you had to wash yourself in segments. First from your waist up. That was the easiest. She always supervised to make sure I did it right. For some reason she was mostly concerned with my ears. Especially behind my ears. Next came what she called "the lower region." I had to sit in the basin to get wet, soap myself then get back in to rinse off. This was the hardest part. No matter how slowly I sat down, there was always a splash, making a mess my mother would have to mop up later. Last came my legs and feet, which always requiring thorough scrubbing. Especially my knees. I am telling you this to make it clear that I was quite certain that the epithet "dirty" was totally incorrect. How could I be a "dirty Jew" after our painstaking daily effort to keep meticulously clean? An effort that my accusers clearly did not always make! I was certain that my hygiene was superior to that of most of the kids—or even adults—hurling insults. It just did not make any sense. So I put it to my father, who knew everything. He became thoughtful, gave me a hug, and sat me on his knee.

"It is a metaphor," he explained. "A metaphor is a way of saying that one thing equals another different thing. It means that no matter how personally clean, clever or good we may be, in their eyes, the Nazis' eyes, all Jews and some others are dirty and stinky and greedy and no good."

I understood then that regardless of who I really was, regardless of what I did or did not do, I belonged to a group of people who were to be avoided, feared, banished, and killed off like rats spreading disease. I understood this because I saw it and heard it everywhere. By age eight, I felt like Alice falling through the Rabbit Hole into a crazy, absurd world where nothing made any sense anymore.

There was little time to ponder this then, but the question in various forms recurred throughout my life and led to a never-ending search for answers. As an adult I continued to make professional choices to combat, then flee, and later attempt to heal insanity, delusions, and cruelty. At first,

Typical Nazi poster of "The Eternal Jew," depicting Jews as evil, menacing, exploitative moneylenders and Communists.

I thought education would do it. Teaching rationality, great ideas, and appreciation of beauty through literature, music, and the fine arts! These things were so very important to me; they taught me how to be human! Surely this was the answer!

Regrettably, I realized as I grew older that most Nazis were not ignorant. They knew all about the props of civilized life. Hitler was a painter. Not a very good one, but a painter. Many of the leaders of the Reich were collectors of the fine arts; indeed, they stole the best of it from all over the world and hung it in their museums and on their walls. They grew up with the best music the human mind could produce, and it did not make any difference. They liked classical music so much they organized an orchestra in Auschwitz made up of inmates. They were distinguished musicians, the crème de la crème, the very best, forced to entertain their captors, their executioners, their torturers, with the heavenly music of Mozart and Beethoven. It boggles the mind.

Sometimes I think my life path has been a long and often futile effort to help roll the heavy rock of violence, ignorance, intolerance, and insanity up the steep mountain, only to watch it roll back once it reaches the top. It seems that evil always finds a way to reassert itself. The good news is that so does its opposite.

4. From Paradise to Purgatory to Hell

When I first read *The Divine Comedy*, I was amazed, enchanted, and incredulous. It was beautiful, fascinating, dangerous, and naïve all at the same time! The language was sheer music, even in translation. It offered a sense of continuity and hope. Evil and suffering were transcended by poetry and beauty. I loved it, in spite of its being all wrong. As far as I was concerned, the narrative was upside down—it should have been in reverse. It should have started in Paradise, descended through the circles, and ended up in the deepest regions of Hell. For me it certainly did, at least for a while. I got out of Hell somehow, but I never dwelled in Paradise again, not for any length of time. Nor did I have a reliable guide, although some kind of juvenile Virgil may have taken up residence in my soul.

This is what happened.

Soon after I was no longer allowed to go to school, after weeks of high tension in the house, after much whispering and sudden silences the moment I appeared, after my mother and father started yelling and fighting with each other more often than usual about things I could not understand, I woke up one morning to discover the house in chaos and everyone packing feverishly. I was told to gather a few things that were important to me, but they had to fit in a small suitcase I could carry. We could take with us only a few of our belongings and had to leave the rest behind. I chose the only doll I cared about: a small, soft three-month-old baby boy dressed in blue overalls called Pityu, or Pete in English. He had sweet, rosy cheeks and beautiful blue eyes that opened and closed. He wore a hooded terrycloth cardigan over his overalls. The hood was necessary, because he had no hair yet. He was very huggable and I loved him. He was the only doll I ever played with. Pityu was displaced and forgotten in the coming chaotic years, but eighteen years later, when I was searching for a good name for my newborn son, there was no doubt that his name would be Peter. I hadn't made the connection until now. Choosing the books to take was much more difficult. I did not understand why we had to move. And in such a great hurry. Books were my closest, most reliable friends, my constant companions, sometimes the only things that made sense in our topsy-turvy world. I did not want to leave any of them behind.

Father assured me it was all right. "We will be back soon," he said. "This is just a temporary move. We'll be safer staying with Uncle Rezso and Aunt Jeanette. The books will be waiting for you when we come back."

I believed him. He had never lied to me before, but he was mistaken, both about the books and about being back soon.

I remember the day when we left our home only vaguely. I do remember, though, my ongoing longing for the balcony where I had spent blissful afternoons in the company of great minds and souls: the poets, novelists, and philosophers channeled through the books, populating my universe. They talked to me about the wonders and beauty of the world. They spoke of freedom, kindness, love, and the meaning of existence. They seemed more present then many actual people in my life. Amazingly, they stayed with me even after I had to leave the physical books behind. I only vaguely remember saying goodbye to the beautiful garden with the fruit trees I liked to climb, the birds I liked to watch, the hills I loved to roam. But I can clearly remember the sadness and the pain and the nameless anxiety about dislocation and the uncertain, unimaginable future. The only thing I knew with any certainty, although I didn't understand it, was that Jews were no longer allowed to live in Buda.

Starting in April 1944, an edict required every Hungarian Jew over the age of six to wear a bright yellow six-sided star—made of silk, cloth, or velvet, measuring 10x19 centimeters—sewn into their garments on the upper left-hand side of their chest. In June 1944, it was declared that all Jews must be moved to designated "starred houses" in Pest. There weren't any in Buda. This had to be—and was —accomplished in ten days! Non-compliance was deadly.

In retrospect, I should have been better prepared. For months, visitors—both friends and strangers I had never seen before—came and went much more frequently than usual. They talked with my parents in hushed tones and went quiet when I appeared. I was sent outside to play instead of being included in the conversations, which was also unusual. Visitors departed with packages and "gifts." Mother was crying a lot. I understood later that my parents were asking friends, even Margit, to protect some of our valuables, to take them for safekeeping. Margit could not come with us to the Jewish House in Pest. She could no longer work for Jews. She returned to the countryside, to the village she came from, to live with her sister and their family. We moved in with Uncle Rezso and Aunt Jeanette. I did not know it, but it was the first of many moves that came to define my existence from then on—even throughout most of my adult life. I did not know it was merely one more stop on the road to Hell. It was just as well.

Sigmund Freud, another Jew, who by that time had already fled his native Vienna, said, "To endure life is the first duty of all living beings. Illusion can have no value, if it makes this more difficult for us." There is some truth in this. Clarity is good when it can be used for foresight, for avoiding danger, but it can be a great hindrance when you are helplessly stuck in the middle of disaster. For the child "me" at that time, each step, each loss, seemed finite, discrete, something to learn to live with, to adjust to, until better things came. I did not see where it was leading. Few of us did, and those who did kept quiet or freaked out! I did not want to freak out, and for the most part I didn't. I did learn, however, that denial is the universal defense mechanism of the victim. There came a time, after the war ended, when I was in my teens, when I refused to be a victim again. Not that it helped—in fact it made things worse—but at least it preserved my sense of integrity and self-esteem.

Dohany Street 68 still stands, in Pest's VIIth District, at the edge of what was once the ghetto. It is a four-story building built in 1893 in the "eclectic" style. A solid, imposing building in spite of neglect, crumbling masonry, and damages suffered during the bombardments and long siege of Budapest. In 1944, it was unmarred and well-maintained. It had massive balconies with balustrades facing the busy downtown street and an impressive, heavy entrance gate replete with columns and stone ornaments. The apartment building was built around a courtyard that was encased by a gangway on each floor. The gangways had impressive wrought-iron protective barriers and were paved with mosaic tile chips. The high-ceilinged apartments generally had three bedrooms, a spacious living room, a rear kitchen, a bath, and a tiny toilet opening from the hall. Quite adequate for the average upscale urban family. It was far from adequate for four-plus families and numerous transients crowded together, which was the situation after it was declared a starred house by the Fascist Government. All in all, ten adults and I lived in a space where before there were only two people. We had a system with tight time limits on using the one bathroom and the single lavatory. You could only pray that you did not develop stomach upsets or other emergencies. Needless to say, the apartment was noisy and crowded. The women often fought over the meager resources, food, and the use of the kitchen and bathroom privileges.

There were a great many starred houses around us. Dohany 68, like all Jewish Houses, had a huge illuminated Star of David erected above the entrance gate. We were ready targets; nobody could miss us. Exactly what the authorities wanted. Some Jewish families chose to go into hiding at this point, but Father thought it less risky to obey orders. When you were discovered hiding, you were shot on the spot or deported to a concentration camp. That's what happened to Anne Frank and her family. They were betrayed by a neighbor while in hiding. They all perished in camp, except for her father, who managed to preserve her diary.

Building designated for Jews in Pest, just like ours, 1944.

Every day, or so it seemed, new restrictions emerged. For a week or so, Mother and the other women diligently cut out large stars of David from bright yellow cloth sold expressly for that purpose. They had to be the prescribed size and were hand-sewn with large stitches onto our coats, dresses, and every other garment we wore in public. It was now illegal to leave the house without the star clearly visible, and even then, we could go out only at designated times and to designated places. It was dangerous for Jews to be on the streets even during official times. The Yellow Star became our Scarlet Letter, for all to see. It made us a ready target and we were often pushed around, attacked and sworn at. It was also intended to make us feel ashamed and humiliated. Instead, I felt angry, defiant, and resentful. Not that there were many outlets for such feelings under the circumstances, so I had to invent small symbolic acts of defiance doable for a nine-year-old. The Cherry Caper was one of these.

One day I was presented with a small bowl of fresh red cherries. I have no idea who got hold of them or how. It seemed a miracle. Food was scarce, especially fresh fruit. How I cherished those cherries! I still remember the tart sweetness, or sweet tartness, and the elastic texture and glorious wine color of the fruit. I did not want to waste any of it. I saved the pits and put them to good use. Crouching behind the balustrades of our third story balcony, I could survey the scene below on the busy street through the narrow gaps between the concrete columns without being seen or suspected. This afforded me a strategic position, or so I thought. With the dedication of a sharpshooter, I took careful aim. I chose my targets carefully from passers-by in uniform and those wearing an Arrow Cross or Nazi armband. I had to be picky; I had only so many cherry pits. It was tricky, especially when there was a breeze, but I seldom missed. I found great solace and amusement in the bewildered looks of my "victims." They never knew what hit them, or where it came from. It was not a particularly effective retribution, nor was it a wise thing to do, but I had fun.

There were quite a few children in the building and we hung out together when we could. We played hide-and-go-seek in the dark, musty stairwells, as we were not allowed to go outside and only very seldom into the courtyard. I think I had a crush on one of the boys, Peter R, or perhaps it was the other way around. It is hard to tell now. In any case, he was a couple of years older—quick, funny, with a sweet grin and shiny blond hair. One day someone gave me a small red gingerbread heart. It was beautiful, a real treasure. I made the mistake of showing it off. Peter gave me a chase for it. He was bigger and quicker and eventually snatched it out of my hand. I was reduced to running after him, shouting, "Give me back my heart! It is mine!" He just laughed. Everyone laughed. I did not understand why. I was young and naïve. I don't remember if I ever got my heart back. Perhaps he still has it if he survived the Holocaust. I never saw him again after we left the Dohany Street House.

It was not just my heart that I was losing; sometimes I thought I was losing my mind as well. I was always, always aware of the danger of losing my life, our lives, in an instant. In those crowded, dark surroundings, I yearned for the bright, open spaces of the Buda hills. I was often engulfed in restless longing for sunshine and freedom. My parents understood, but could not help me.

Then, one hot summer Sunday, visitors arrived. This was a rare occurrence. People did not visit starred houses. It was frowned upon; it was dangerous. These visitors could and did take a chance. One of them wore the uniform of an officer of the Wehrmacht, the German Army. The House panicked. The Wehrmacht was not considered as deadly as the SS, but German military—any military really—meant trouble, big trouble. However, this visitor meant no harm. He turned out to be the new boyfriend of beautiful Livia, who had been my father's assistant in saner days before the German occupation when Father had a dental practice. They brought food, friendship, and hope. They noted the trapped heat, the lack of ventilation, the crowded, unsanitary conditions. They saw the longing in my eyes. They offered to take me out without my yellow star, so we could go to a nice place. Jews were not allowed in nice places. I loved Livia and trusted Mr. Boyfriend, let's call him "Sebastian," in spite of his uniform.

"Please Dad, please! Sebastian is a German officer, he'll protect me," I pleaded.

I felt desperate to pretend that I was a normal person even just for a short while. My father reluctantly agreed. We all knew it was dangerous.

Livia and Sebastian took me to one of my favorite outdoor swimming pools on the beautiful grounds of the Grand Hotel Gellert in Buda, nestled under the hills by the Danube. It was a special treat to go there, because the pool was fed by natural spring water and had (and still has) a wave machine that imitated the ocean. It was a popular place and there were many people there. As soon as we got into our bathing suits, even before we spread our blankets on the grass, I took a running jump into the artificial surf and imagined that I was swimming across the ocean toward freedom. I had never ever swum in the ocean. Hungary is landlocked.

I felt like a visitor from the Underworld. I soaked up the sunshine and savored the gentle embrace of the water. People around us were eating, laughing, seemingly without a care in the world. It was a peaceful scene, as though the war did not exist, as though the air raid sirens would never sound again. For the first time in many months, which felt like eternity, I was utterly relaxed, grateful for the gift of freedom, fresh air, hope, and happiness. An illusion, of course, but it felt very real for an hour or so. Then everything changed. The light shifted and a chilling sense of danger materialized out of nowhere. Something was wrong. I scanned my surroundings and did not register anything out of the ordinary, yet the need to get out of there became overwhelming. Reluctantly I asked to be taken home. I could not give a reason and I did not want to go home, yet I could not stay. I felt embarrassed, foolish. The adults responded to my tone of urgency and unease, and we left abruptly. It turned out to be a good thing. Sebastian later found out that less than fifteen minutes later, police scoured the pool area demanding identifications. They were looking for a trespassing Jewish girl. A good, law-abiding citizen had recognized me and called the authorities. The public had to be protected against the contaminating presence of a Jewish child. It was the end of my clandestine outings for a while. I was nine years old at the time.

Now I was stuck back in Dohany St. Dohany means tobacco in Hungarian and all the adults there smoked cigarettes. Unfiltered ones for men and filtered ones for women, when they were available. Smoking kept them sane. More or less. They often chose cigarettes over food and suffered greatly when neither was available. Food was now rationed for everyone in the city. By the time we, the Yellow Star people, were allowed in the stores, there was often nothing left. In order to eat, we relied on the black market if we had money or jewelry to sell or barter, or on the goodwill and sacrifice of outside friends. I was fortunate, because I don't remember actually going hungry during this time. I did not have much of an appetite to begin with and my parents made sure that I ate, even if they didn't. Food acquired tremendous value. It became the universal currency, and I have never again taken it for granted to this day. Tea and coffee were more precious than gold and were sold and measured out on precision scales, until they disappeared altogether.

My uncle had one of these scales in his dental supply store for selling fine gold chips used for filling teeth. The store was now part of the apartment, used as additional living space. It had built-in counters and display cabinets containing packets of Novocain capsules, wax, spooky molds for taking impressions, false porcelain teeth of all shades, amalgam and other materials for filling cavities, drills and bits and prongs for pulling teeth, and other miscellaneous items, whose mysterious functions I could not even guess. I was glad we did not have to sleep there.

Misery continued to accelerate on many levels. The whole city became the target of Allied air raids. The air raid sirens now shrieked their warnings both night and day. The idea was to give ten to fifteen minutes' warning to run for shelter, but soon the bombs started falling immediately. It was like the game of musical chairs. At the sound of the sirens you would drop whatever you were doing, wherever you were, and dive into the closest shelter. It was an eerie sight when the busy streets of the capital suddenly emptied, streetcars and buses stopped, and people ran in all directions seeking admittance to buildings, seeking cover. When the all clear sounded, many of those buildings were burning and significantly fewer people were alive.

Those who could escaped to the countryside. We could not. It turned out that this was actually a good thing. Why? Because while you escaped most of the air raids, artillery fire, intense combat, and famine, you were much more likely to be killed in the concentration camps. I only mention this to make clear a principal lesson I learned early on: conventional methods of decision-making and risk-taking become largely irrelevant in times of extreme crisis, when the whole world turns upside down, topsy-turvy, chaotic, insane. At times like this, the old rules of the game, whatever they were, no longer applied. You had to improvise and hope for the best. You also had to be prepared for the worst.

Our cellar in Dohany Street, a coal cellar, was dark, damp, crowded, and cold. It was lit intermittently by a few precious candles when absolutely necessary. For the most part we huddled in the dark, wrapped in blankets and sitting on stacked wood or the odd stool. As the explosions drew closer, we physically felt the approach of danger in our tense muscles and upset stomachs. When the bombs were getting closer, we felt the whole building shake, as in a direct hit. My father and most able-bodied men would rush out to look for fires on the roof or elsewhere and extinguish them wherever they popped up. We had buckets of water at strategic points for that purpose. I joined them whenever I had the chance, against my mother's protests. It helped me to be active, do something useful, and escape the dark and crowded nether regions of the house, where infants and children cried, the sick moaned, and panic was ever present.

I remember how guilty I felt for feeling relieved that we were not the ones hit, knowing that another building was hit and that people had died there. More than that, those of us who prayed, prayed that we would be spared, that someone else would be the victim. I, too, asked the powers-that-be for the bombs to spare us, for them to fall elsewhere. I think I am still trying to atone for those days, those built-in primitive instincts of self-preservation.

Food, electricity, and fuel were now in increasingly short supply. Bread and other basic essentials were largely unavailable, even as rations. The windows had to be sheathed with heavy, dark blinds and black cloth. Not a glimmer of light was allowed to be visible from the outside. Neighboring houses were raided and the inhabitants shot, accused of being spies and "signaling the enemy." Each of us had a small carryall with essentials—underwear, an extra sweater, medicine, water and some food—a survival kit we could grab at short notice. We never knew when we might be evacuated from the building. Every night we had to lay out our clothes for the same reason. We didn't have time to grope in the dark when the bombs started to fall. There was absurd, incomprehensible danger everywhere. Bombs fell randomly; they did not discriminate. They might kill us, but they also held up hope for liberation. The murderous humans below were targeting us for no other reason than that we were born Jewish.

Laughter became a very rare commodity, so I was surprised when during yet another middle-of-the-night air raid I was greeted in the cellar with unaccustomed hoots. I was still half asleep and it took me a while to realize that a hanger was protruding through my shirt collar. My mother was apparently extra-careful when she laid out my clothes in the evening that I wouldn't appear all wrinkled in the shelter.

The men in the house organized themselves and took turns on sentry duty in a small cubby hole half-hidden at the bottom of the stairs near the entrance. It used to be the concierge's observation post. They had a shortwave radio, strictly illegal and punishable by execution on the spot. They listened to BBC and Voice of America broadcasts and monitored Allied progress. This was essential for preserving a measure of morale. We might be powerless to fight, but at least could hope to be rescued eventually, that we would survive. There was a map of Europe on the wall studded with small flags representing the moving front lines. It could all be hidden in a matter of seconds when a "lookout" signaled approaching danger. Some of us children volunteered to serve as couriers to alert folks in the house. When danger did approach, this gave everyone a few more precious minutes to prepare, gather some food and water, don warm clothing, and stuff small cherished possessions into their pockets.

One day, a band of Arrow Cross thugs, the Hungarian Nazis, entered the building. We were rounded up, and they checked that no one hid or stayed behind. We were marched through the icy streets for several hours with our hands held high above our heads. Men, women, children, the old, and the sick, all of us with our hands held straight up in surrender. Bystanders gathered to jeer, hurl insults, and grab whatever they could off our bodies. Scarves, gloves, anything…I remember one or two faces with compassion in their eyes. They too were powerless to change anything. It was very hard to keep up the pace. My parents told me I mustn't slow down or drop my arms. Those who did were beaten and shot. I wanted to run, but there was nowhere to go. In addition to the armed guards, we were surrounded by a hostile crowd. I worried about my father. He was not in good health and I could see he was struggling.

After what seemed an interminable time, we were herded into the Great Synagogue at the far end of Dohany Street, the street we lived on. We must have been marched in a great loop around the district. The Synagogue was then, and is once again, a great architectural landmark, a beautiful building dedicated to prayer and the worship of a civilized God. It was then teeming with terrified, dehumanized humanity. We huddled together with hardly any room to stand. We were exhausted and hungry and thirsty and terrified. We were not allowed to move around, even to relieve ourselves. Periodically, the armed guards took away groups of people and replaced them with new arrivals. Rumors circulated. We were all going to be taken to an abandoned brick factory where we would be loaded on freight trains and taken to Auschwitz. We all knew about Aus-

Hungarian Jews waiting for the gas chamber.

chwitz by then. We knew we would die there.

My memories are getting hazy at this point. I don't remember how long we stayed at the Temple waiting for death. It was a long time, perhaps days, without food and water. Time stood still, the world faded into unreality while we clung to each other in desperation. Then, unexpectedly and without any perceptible reason, something extraordinary happened. We were told to go home, back to the starred house, to Dohany Street 68. We were incredulous at first, thinking it was a trick, a cruel deception. Then, one by one at first, then in increasing numbers, people began to leave. No one stopped them. It was for real: we were allowed to go. Being back at the starred house now seemed like a privilege!

We did not know why we were rounded up and we did not know why we were let go. Life was no longer comprehensible. Later, decades later, we discovered that we owed our lives to someone called Raoul Wallenberg, who was later killed by our Soviet "liberators."

5. Endgame No. 1

It seems droll that returning to Dohany Street seemed to us the Great Escape. We rejoiced at being allowed to go "home." Home? Did it really take such a short time to consider the starred house home? Yes, we had escaped mortal danger for the moment. But only for the moment, a very brief moment. We were still crowded together in a house marked by a giant Star of David at the edge of what soon became the ghetto. We were still at the mercy of Nazi raids, deportations, and daily brutality—we were cattle in a pen waiting for the slaughterhouse. In retrospect, the very idea of escape was a chimera that allowed us to go on, to continue, if only for the moment—yet another manifestation of the principle that illusions are often necessary and should be considered a blessing…

My mother had no such illusions and despaired. Father sprang into action. He finally saw our plight was not a temporary aberration. We were not displaced, robbed, imprisoned, and crowded together in marked houses temporarily and for our own protection, as the Nazis maintained. He realized that war's end was getting closer, but it was not yet close enough. Perhaps he had known all along, how could he not? How could anyone not have known? Perhaps it was simply not possible to believe the unbelievable. I don't know. I will never know. I only know that at this point he could have thrown up his hands, rolled over, given up. Many did. Instead, he became determined to get us out of Dohany Street, out of the ghetto—which seemed impossible. Thankfully, Father was good at the Impossible. Much better than at mundane everyday tasks.

To be fair, he probably had been working to find an escape route of some kind for quite a while, hesitating, weighing the best odds for survival, until finally the Synagogue incident forced his hand.

This is what happened.

Father managed to secure "Letters of Protection" for the whole family. Not just for Mother and me, but also for my grandfather, two uncles, and Rezso's wife Jeanette. The Letters of Protection looked impressive and official, and they were ostensibly from the Spanish Embassy! They said that we would reside in a house with other Jews under the protection of the sovereign "neutral" country of Spain where we were off limits to both the Hungarian Arrow Cross and the SS. These letters were hard to come by; you had to have the right connections. They cost a lot of money. I don't know how much exactly, but it depleted everyone's hidden resources and then some. Naturally, they were fake. I don't think Father knew this, but he might have suspected. Remember that, as far as anyone knew, General Franco's Spain was in Hitler's camp.

I found out later—much, much later—that the whole scheme was hatched by a charming Italian adventurer by the name of Giovanni Perlasca. He impressed the Spanish Ambassador, whose wife was Jewish, with his fake credentials. Perlasca arranged safe passage for the Ambassador and his family out of Budapest using money from the fake affidavits bought by Jews to protect themselves. In turn, Perlasca was named acting ambassador. It was a crazy scheme, possible only in those chaotic times. Thank God for graft! It saved many lives. It still does.

The whole scheme was bound to collapse sooner rather than later, and it did, but Father bought some time for us to avoid deportations. We stayed out of the common garden-variety ghetto and were placed instead in the euphemistically designated International Ghetto—international because several European embassies established Protected Houses in the area between Pozsonyi Street and St. Istvan Park, where we landed. Swedish and Spanish affidavits were considered the safest. The Swiss issued too many of them, and they became the first to be suspected and dismissed by the Nazis. Finding ourselves in the Spanish House seemed to us like winning the lottery.

If all this sounds fantastic, even absurd, I have made my point. By the age of ten I had learned some crucial lessons about life and survival.

These are just a few of them:

- Chance and timing rule supreme.
- Buying time when things go bad is one of the most important keys to survival.
- Savor the unmitigated joy when it happens, but savor it cautiously and stay alert, because it will be followed more often than not by additional disaster, pain, and renewed struggle.
- The unpredictable often trumps the predictable, but not always. Rules change so swiftly and often that it is almost impossible to stay ahead of the game.
- Never try to understand good fortune; grab it as it passes.
- Evil is a contagious disease. Decent people can turn into savages at short notice and without warning.
- Altruism and goodness can and do pop up unexpectedly, seemingly out of nowhere, even under the most dire circumstances.

Sometimes I feel that the rest of my long life has been spent trying to understand and assimilate these early experiences.

Back to the bleak and rainy day in 1944 when we said our brief goodbyes to those who remained in Dohany Street. We knew that soon they were going to be forced to move to the ghetto. We each packed up our few belongings: blankets, one or two tattered sweaters, coats, underwear, warm socks (with holes in them since we did not have the time or yarn to mend them), precious soap, toothbrushes, and whatever food we had left. We made bundles from the sheets and blankets to carry things; there was no room for suitcases anymore. We must have looked like a nomadic tribe wandering in the desert. The Hungarian soldiers herded us, bundles on our backs, across town to our new "home." The soldiers were there to make sure no one disappeared, but they also provided some protection from the armed and murderous Arrow Cross gangs that roamed the city on the lookout for Jews to kill and abuse. That was their mission, their job, and the whole purpose of their lives.

The trip from Dohany Street to St. Istvan Park felt like a dangerous adventure, an expedition across the jungle dodging predators that were waiting to devour us ready to attack us. Come to think of it, this was not far from the truth. We walked in silence, trying to keep up. Falling behind was not an option. Nobody spoke. I had a heightened awareness of my surroundings. Everybody was on high alert. We had an instinctive sense of approaching danger, ready to switch to flight mode at a moment's notice. We were transformed into wild animals, a herd of zebra or wildebeests finding their way to a safe watering hole, closing ranks and relying on speed for protection against lurking predators that were waiting to devour us. It seemed to me a long time before we arrived at our new "home." Sigh of relief, we made it to the watering hole. There was not much water in it, nor was the water clear and wholesome. Still, it was a watering hole. For now.

St. Istvan Park and Pozsonyi Street were situated in a newer section of Pest, in Lipotvaros, an area originally favored by affluent, progressive, middle-class Jews. These streets ran parallel to the Danube. The buildings on St. Istvan Park faced it directly, separated from the river by a narrow strip of landscaped "parkland." No. 25 was the building at the end of the L-shaped development. We were the foot of the L with a full view of all that was happening the length of the waterfront. This soon proved to be a mixed blessing.

No. 25 was relatively modern, like most buildings in the area. It was a six-story high-rise with elevators, central heating, and small modern bathrooms with showers. The rooms were smaller, the ceilings lower than in traditional buildings, but there were plenty of windows to let sunshine in. The cellars were small, used mostly for storage and, to a lesser extent, for fuel for the furnace. When they had to serve as air raid shelters, they could not accommodate the absurdly swollen population of the building.

There were no fireplaces or individual heating units in the apartments. When central heating was off during electricity outages, there were no other sources of heat. It was winter and we were very cold most of the time. The deep underground cellar that served as our air raid shelter was frigid. Our fingers and toes turned blue; they froze in spite of socks, gloves and, by now, threadbare shoes. Not surprisingly, I now have arthritis in my fingers despite later treatments. We were required to take cover there when the sirens signaled and stay until the all clear sounded. I tried to stay out of the cellar as much as I could, whenever I could, which was not often enough.

There were good reasons for this. It was much worse even than the cellar in Dohany Street. It was overflowing with suffering, unwashed, starving humanity fighting for a place to hide, a place to feel safe. Babies were hungry and crying, the sick were moaning and sometimes dying unnoticed. The doctors among us did their best, but there was no medicine and soon no sanitation to speak of. There were rats competing for morsels of food when they were available, which was seldom since we were all starving. I can still smell the odor of mold, panic, and human decay permeating everything. The best description I can think of can be found in *The Lower Depths* by Dostoevsky, which I read a few years later. It is about a different time, a different place, different people, and different oppression, but suffering is suffering: timeless, senseless, physical, a disease of the body and the soul.

Once again, the extraordinary became the norm and the unthinkable, the expected. We did not imagine that living conditions could deteriorate any further, but they did. Even upstairs, outside the cellar shelter, five or more extended families were crowded into each small apartment. People fought over the few beds, some of which were taken over by whole families. The rest of us slept on the crowded floors, like sardines in a can. I staked out a place for myself under the piano left behind by the original inhabitants. No one contested it, because I was the only one small enough to fit. I felt safer there. Nobody could step on me. It was a lucky choice.

As I write this, I am aware of an increasing reluctance to revisit these final few months before the end of the war. I was old enough to remember and my memories are clear and powerful, but they are episodic. I can only see the faces of my own family. The rest of the crowded humanity with whom I shared the apartment, the house, and the cellar remains a blur. I don't remember their names. I could not recognize even one of them. I wish I could. Here are fragments of rescued memories—mostly about food and fear.

In the beginning, we had potatoes and beans. When those were gone, there were lentils. Lentils keep forever. I disliked lentils, but it was better than starving. Today I never touch lentils if I can help it, healthy as they may be. After the lentils were gone, there was mostly nothing. Sometimes the men would venture out to forage and bring back chunks of horsemeat when they heard through the grapevine that a horse had been killed by shrapnel, artillery fire, or some other explosion. It tasted nauseatingly sweet and reminded me of rotting flesh, of the corpses abandoned on the streets. I could not touch it, no matter how hungry I was, and at this point even I was permanently hungry. The rest of the city was hurting too—food rationed and the stores open only a few hours a day. Jews were not allowed out during those hours. People fought over scraps of food.

I volunteered to go to a nearby bakery that was open a few hours a day, since I did not "look" particularly Jewish and I was a nine-year-old. I did not wear a star. People took pity on me. There were lines in the bakery, but sometimes people let me go ahead because they saw I was hungry. Kindness shines and is remembered when everything else is darkness. The bread, when I was lucky enough to get it, was coarse, dark, and barely edible; nevertheless, it was greeted with relief and delight back at the house. We shared it with as many as possible. Every crumb was precious. I remember the happy satisfaction and pride I felt. It still feels like one of the biggest accomplishments of my life. We were also thirsty much of the time. There was no running water in the building, nor in most of the city by this time. The men organized convoys to bring containers of precious fresh water from God knows where. It was dangerous, but by then everything was very dangerous. Many did not come back alive from these forays.

After almost constant bombardment, the city was encircled by Soviet troops. Fewer bombs fell, but artillery fire took their place. The German troops kept on fighting. They knew they were doomed, but they still kept on fighting, burning and destroying everything in their path. They blew up all the bridges across the Danube and destroyed whatever infrastructure remained after the air raids. They were determined to destroy what was left of the city and its inhabitants, determined to leave a wasteland behind.

Their first priority was, as always, killing Jews. You might think they had more urgent tasks to attend to at this point, like running for their lives. Instead they were determined, with the enthusiastic help of the native Hungarian Arrow Cross thugs, to finish the task of cleansing the world of us. I think it was a recreational activity for them, a way to prove how powerful they were, on the brink of losing all power—even as they were becoming the Hunted themselves.

Several days a week, from our window I saw people lined up on the banks of the river surrounded by guards. Men, women, and children—hundreds of them. I could not distinguish their features from a distance. For hours and hours, I saw them every time I looked out. Then suddenly they were gone. Disappeared. Nobody ever saw them leave.

If you visit Budapest, beautiful rebuilt Budapest, walk down to the banks of the Danube and look at the shoes. There are shoes of all sizes and styles scattered about in random but well-designed patterns. Walking shoes, baby shoes, lace-ups, boots, and even shoes with heels. They are made of bronze and cast iron. They are grippingly beautiful, the originals long gone. They belonged to the people shot and dumped into the river. The Nazis, ever sensible, made them take off their shoes before they killed them.

Nobody told me this at the time, but it became very clear that our Protected Houses were not all that well protected. The owners of those shoes by the Danube were all from the Protected Houses. Swiss houses were the earliest casualties. The militia appeared, usu-

ally at daybreak, and "took" the inhabitants. They searched the buildings for anyone trying to hide. They shot on sight those who ran or hid. We all knew we would be next. The embassies were gone as was any idea of "protection."A pervasive sense of doom and dread enveloped our community. Father steadfastly held on to hope. Every day, liberation came closer. Every explosion, every air raid, every hit by the Soviet artillery brought closer the end of the madness of WWII. We

Top: Jews lined up by the Danube to be shot.
Below: The dead waiting to be thrown into the river.

might or might not survive, but it would come. I knew he was right and it gave me strength to hold on, the strength to avoid the contagion of the overwhelming fear, horror, and anxiety that stretched their dark wings over us. Not entirely, but enough.

Budapest now lay in ruins. Our building still stood, a miracle, although it was severely damaged and pockmarked by bullets. Many of the outside walls had been blown off by artillery hits and all the windows were shattered or gone altogether. The cellar became more crowded than ever. The cannons stopped targeting us because the fighting now progressed street by street. Wherever we looked we were surrounded by the dead.

One day in early April, there was a brief lull in the fighting. Some of us went upstairs to the second-floor apartment we shared with many others for a break from the dark, crowded horror of the cellar. We needed light and fresh air to feel human, no matter how briefly. Father, Grandfather, my uncle, my aunt, and I, and perhaps some others, gathered in the room with the big window, the room with the piano where I slept. Suddenly there was the unmistakable sound of celebration from the neighboring building mixed with the distant noises of war. People were shouting and hollering with joy and relief in the building perpendicular to us. We could see and hear them clearly, since their windows were facing our windows. This was astounding. We were not accustomed to sounds of joy, and we had forgotten the sounds of celebration.

Then someone shouted, "There are Soviet soldiers on the street! It is all over! We have survived. The Germans are gone!"

We began to hug, laugh, shout, and cry. Someone ran to tell the others. Relief, joy, and gratitude enveloped us.

It was then that the grenade exploded. The room became a swirling black hole with darting red lights piercing the darkness. I instinctively ducked under the piano. I knew I mustn't move. The world slowed down; it was coming to an end. I heard screams, then it was quiet. When the dust cleared, I saw my father lying on the floor, bleeding profusely. He could not move. My uncle and aunt were also wounded, though not quite as severely as it later turned out. Father recovered eventually, but he never again walked without a cane and without pain. I was unharmed and so was my grandfather. The oldest and the youngest.

6. Liberation: The False Spring

We soon found that our liberators were dangerous in their own right: jumpy, confused, and trigger-happy. They were in enemy territory, still fighting a bloody siege on the other side of the Danube, in Buda, wary of being ambushed. They could not easily distinguish between friend and foe. They did not particularly like Jews, or at least most of them didn't. Many of us were naïve enough and hurt enough to expect to be greeted with open arms, embraced, and comforted as long-suffering victims of Nazi persecution. We were in for a rude awakening. It did not happen.

We were treated with suspicion, just like everyone else. The troops were hungry, just as we were, so they took whatever food they could find, their rations being in short supply. They were on the lookout for valuables, and looting was common. For reasons I still find mysterious, they were particularly interested in watches. Perhaps the ability to measure time made them feel safer—a reassurance of being alive and present? They would demand "Chas, Chas, Chas" (watch) and relieve anyone they encountered of their wristwatch, as well as other valuables, none too gently. Most soldiers were very young—sixteen, seventeen, or eighteen—and came from remote regions of the Soviet Union. They were not used to Western lifestyles and amenities. Many had never seen indoor plumbing. They had fought their way through Europe, suffering terrible casualties. Stray bullets were still flying in Pest and a full-scale war continued to rage in Buda. None of this encouraged friendly open interactions.

Word got out that women, especially young girls, were not safe. The troops were starved for sex. My mother dressed me in what would qualify today as rags, which was not too difficult under the circumstances. She covered my head with a "babushka," a headscarf that hid my hair and most of my face. She did the same for herself.

Aunt Juci magically appeared one sunny day in the spring. She had gotten word that we had survived and was eager to offer us shelter and share whatever remained of her home. Being Christian, she had been allowed to stay in her apartment and she managed to stay alive during the allied air raids and subsequent siege.

What happened next is something of a blur. I know we crossed town on foot to Wesselenyi ucca. Pest was unrecognizable. The pavements were torn up most of the way, so we had to clamber over heaps of rubble of boulders and torn up asphalt. Skeletons of buildings destroyed by bombs and fire lined the streets, not one of them intact. I remember upended carriages with dead horses still attached to them. I averted my gaze from the dead humans littering the streets. I still feel the visceral dread and my inability to process the sights. It was the stuff of nightmares to come. I could cope with clear and present danger, I could cope with hunger and fear, but I could not cope with the dead. Part of my soul is still wandering in that lunar landscape of death and destruction illuminated by a clueless sunshine. The walk from Hell back to Earth was a very long walk.

Juci and Zoli's apartment at Wesselenyi ucca 51 was four stories high. Zoli and Juci lived on the third floor. When we finally arrived there, everything looked unfamiliar. Part of the building was not there anymore. The apartment was where it used to be, sort of. The stairwell was more or less intact. The gangway, the kitchen facing it, and the long narrow entrance hall looked familiar. The living room seemed livable, except for the shattered, broken windows, which were covered with cardboard. Some of the walls had deep cracks in them. The door on the left leading to a large bedroom was locked. "Don't go there," my mother shouted when I tried to open it. She sounded terrified.

Typical scene in Budapest after the war ended in April 1945

The locked door led nowhere. I know, because I sneaked up behind Juci when she opened it once and caught a glimpse of what lay beyond it. Three of the walls were still covered with wallpaper in genteel shades of yellow, green, and brown with delicate flowers scattered over it. But the fourth wall was missing. It looked like the stage in a theater. But this was not the theater. It was not make-believe. The fourth wall was sheared off. It led to the Void, to instant death. Then, as now, I often dreamt about stepping through it. Perhaps that's how I will die one day: the door will open and I will step through and perhaps will feel no more pain.

I did not fully realize how much pain and anger have lain hidden in my soul. I thought they were vanquished long ago. I can feel them reemerge as I write this account sixty years later. Therefore, I won't linger.

***

At some point in the summer of 1945 after the War ended and

Peace was declared, the Russian military finally receded out of sight into their respective military installations around the country. Budapest was officially no longer under Russian occupation, but of course it was, only less obviously.

Still, Soviet soldiers no longer roamed freely, and some semblance of normalcy returned to our lives. There was a general election and a new government was formed consisting of a coalition of the Small Landowner's Party, the Social Democrats, and the Communist Party. The Small Landowner's Party was the most conservative and held the majority. We were all hopeful and enthusiastic about the slogans proclaiming the intention to "heal the wounds," rebuild the country, and live in a free democratic society. It never happened. We didn't know it then, but this was to be the last free election for many decades to come.

Budapest was starving again. Money was worthless; inflation was rampant. Peasant farmers saw their opportunity and drove their horse-drawn buggies to town from the countryside. They would only exchange their produce for gold, silver, and precious stones. Most of our possessions were gone or inaccessible. Hunger became an everyday threat. Mother came to the rescue.

Her hands were beautiful. Her tapered fingers were soft and narrow ending in beautifully shaped oval nails. In addition to her wedding band—which I still have—she wore a delicate white gold diamond and sapphire ring. It hugged her finger with graceful grapevine design. It was an object of great beauty. It turned out to be life-giving when it metamorphosed into a hefty geese, flour, sugar, cheese butter, sausages, beans, and potatoes—enough food to sustain us for months. I learned then that when the chips are down, food always trumps gold, silver, and prized possessions. Even though Mother rationed food carefully, it was soon gone. It remained scarce and eating episodic until Father came back from hospital. Though he was still on crutches and struggling to walk, he was somehow able to resume his dental practice in the war-torn city. This provided us with better than average food supply since he was often paid with flour, sugar, eggs, potatoes and the occasional chicken or duck. These were treasures, beyond the value of gold or diamonds. Slowly, gradually life returned to some sort of routine. Margit, our old maid, nanny, cook, and general boss, reemerged from the countryside where she had spent the worst of the war and moved in with us to take care of the house once again. Nobody had any money, and it was pretty useless anyway. Inflation meant that whatever money came your way, you'd better exchange it for goods immediately because by evening it would be pretty much worthless.

A recurring dream during those years had to do with finding myself in a great bright hall with an abundance of gleaming fresh vegetables and fruit of all sorts. I dreamt of oranges and bananas and lemons, exotic fruit I only ever saw in my imagination. I dreamt of sausages, salami, ham, and meats of all sorts, beautiful fresh bread, crisp buns, and chocolate—all sorts of chocolate, plain and with mocha filling and chocolate-covered cherries filled with real rum or cognac—and lots of pastries. More than a decade later when I saw my first supermarket, I thought that I was transported back to my dream world...

We soon left our communal living arrangements with Uncle Zoli and Aunt Juci. Our old home did not exist anymore, but Father found a house, more or less intact, just a few blocks away from our old home in Buda. It was a one-story rancher on the corner of Narcisz and Pagony Street with three bedrooms, a bath, and an additional separate toilet. A veritable palace after the deprivations of the recent past. I loved it at first sight. It sat on a fenced-in corner lot surrounded by mature fruit trees, shrubs, and flower beds brimming with fragrant roses, pink and red and yellow carnations, and dramatic purple and white dahlias. Geraniums bloomed in the window boxes and petunias in all shades of the spectrum (except black) brimmed over their containers by the patio. Farther down at the bottom of the garden, overgrown lilac and jasmine bushes were covered with pink, white, pale blue, and purple flowers, creating a cave of fragrant delight all summer and spring. I could be at peace here, read, study, daydream, and be content.

My room was at the very end of the house. It was long and narrow, divided by an arch into two sections. My bed was on the end by the window overlooking a lovely flowering almond tree. The far end had my desk, bookshelves, and a comfortable chair with a side table. It had both a window with a view of the garden and a miniature balcony above ground level. This meant that I had a private entrance to the garden without my parents being any wiser. I only had to jump off my little private balcony, careful to avoid landing in the narrow stairwell leading to the basement apartment where Margit lived. Luckily, I never missed, and she never told on me.

In the spring I curled up in the curved wrought iron bars protecting my window from intruders. I remember the velvety moonlit nights and the subtle scent of the flowering almond tree nearby working their magic to heal my wounded soul. Life was beautiful again, in spite of everything. I enjoyed many tranquil summer nights stargazing in splendid isolation soothed by the scent of roses, jasmine, and lilac and the vastness of the universe revealed by the stars. My whole being felt the healing energy of ongoing creation surrounding me with beauty, diminishing little by little the wounds inflicted by the war. Diana, the Moon Goddess, protector of wild animals and nature, took care of me. I became one of her wards. I could sense it in my bones. I did not know it at the time, but like her, I too was destined to hunt alone…

We had a large garden with flower beds and vegetable patches. Also four or five hens and a handsome rooster, very full of himself. We had fresh eggs year-round and baby chicks—little golden fluffs of cuddly softness—a couple times a year. On Sundays we had very fresh fried or roasted chicken, but I did not like to think about that, since I knew them all personally. I wished I were a vegetarian, but I did not have the strength of my convictions. My favorite hideaway was the gazebo of tall lilac and jasmine bushes where I read and day-dreamed and did my school work until late in the fall. The scents of flowers blended with streaks of sunshine filtered through the bushes became a source of sheer delight.

My father now needed constant care and assistance due to his injuries, although he graduated from needing crutches to using a cane to get around. He became Mother's full-time job for years to come. Theirs was now a symbiotic relationship; they took care of each other. My father's body was damaged forever, but his spirit remained intact. He reconnected with surviving friends, rebuilt his dental practice, and resumed an active political life promoting the interests of the National Association of Dental Technicians as its President. It was due to his efforts and advocacy that a law was passed for qualified practitioners to maintain independent practices without medical supervision. He was instrumental in developing the standards and curriculum for passing the national qualifying examinations. He was also a respected member of the teaching faculty. Father also found the energy to establish what became the largest, most respected and innovative dental laboratory in the country, employing and training dozens of people. He was a creative but autocratic boss well-loved by most, but he did make enemies. A kind of Bill Gates of his time.

Father believed passionately in democracy and social responsibility. He became a prominent leader in the Social Democratic Party, which was a full member of the coalition government at the time.

My father's activities allowed the family to rebuild and live reasonably comfortably, at least for the next few years. In contrast, my Mother's body remained young and strong with a few exceptions, but her spirit was permanently impaired and she never fully recovered. Her anxiety became more and more pronounced as did her impatience, anger, and intolerance of the roller coaster of our life's trials and tribulations. Her pessimistic nature did not allow her to enjoy the small joys and blessings fate threw our way from time to time. Like Pythia, she foresaw doom long before it arrived; hell, she foresaw doom that never arrived, although in all fairness, much of it did eventually. Her trust in people and a benevolent Universe was shattered forever. A common disease of those surviving the Holocaust, or even other less severe experiences.

Settled in our new home, I thought I was ready to start school in September of 1945. At that time, Hungary had two parallel educational paths: academic and technical. You had to make the choice by fifth grade and your grades had to support it. Your social standing and family connections were not immaterial either. I entered the rarefied adolescent world of the Gimnasium. Szilagyi Erzsebet was an eight-year college preparatory program, the equivalent of a lycée in France.

School started before we moved back to Buda. I had to commute from Pest using public transportation such as it was for the first few months. Returning to school after the War, after the Holocaust, was not easy for me. I don't think it was for any of us. I had just turned eleven years old, but felt much, much older.

The Gimnazium was in the XIIth district just on the other side of the Danube from Pest and the Alagut, a tunnel blasted through the Castle cliffs of Buda. From Pest, you had to cross the Chainbridge or "Lanchid" to get there. It was the first suspension bridge in Europe, built by a British engineer. It was blasted to smithereens by the Nazis and we had to use a temporary pontoon bridge until it was rebuilt. I was always slightly apprehensive taking the bus across the mysterious interior of the Tunnel illuminated only by flickering electrical lighting that might give up at any time. The urban landscape strongly resembled an archeological site in Pompeii or the Acropolis. Houses still standing were interspersed with empty, weed-infested spaces strewn with fragments of bricks and boulders where houses, schools, libraries, and hospitals had once stood. Roads and pavements on the way to school were torn and surviving structures were pockmarked by bullet holes. The scenery was now part of our everyday lives, and soon it lost its power to shock.

School was too far away to ride my bike. Nobody had a car in those days, so I had to use public transportation, which meant a bus in the Buda hills. Buses were always crowded, but it was the

My mother and me, circa 1947

worst during rush hour. More often than not we could not get inside but were stuck on the outside steps. This was called "hanging on" because we hung onto the door handles and rails thoughtfully provided for that purpose. It was a bit risky and therefore kind of fun. We would hang on for dear life and scream gleefully whenever the

Aerial view of Budapest with the bridges over the Danube blown up by the retreating German army.

bus sped up, stopped suddenly, or took a sharp turn. In winter, our fingers went numb in the windy cold and it was hard to keep holding on. It may not be coincidental that I never developed a taste for roller coasters.

Still, I preferred "hanging on" to being squished inside like sardines swaying this way and that, because I was not yet tall enough to reach the handles overhead. There were never any seats left by the time I got on, and if by some miracle there was one, the children were required to give up their seats to the next adult female or elderly person entering the bus. By the time I was twelve, I was fully developed and this created additional problems in the crowded bus. I got to be very good at spotting and avoiding the proximity of men who would be likely to take advantage of the crowded conditions by groping and invading my privacy. I may have been fully developed physically, but totally uninterested and generally ignorant about sex. Even in non-abusive situations, I hated to be touched until quite late in my teens and preferred to be admired from a distance.

That first year in school was an uneasy reunion of our damaged generation. We all had our own personal traumas, our losses, our stories of survival, but they stayed well-hidden. We did not talk about it. It seemed that we had this extraordinary tacit agreement to avoid any mention of the recent past. It seemed enough that we were there, that we survived. We needed a chance for a clean start, a rebirth, so we could establish a measure of trust and acceptance of each other, based on the present, not burdened by the knowledge of whether our families were the hunters, the hunted, or fellow travelers during the war years. We did not want to rehash our suffering, our losses. We were young, we were exuberant, we felt invincible. Having escaped death, we celebrated life! Well, most of us anyway…I find it amazing that we never lost our ability for creative mischief and fun. It became a challenge, a necessity, to make the most of our lives. Or at least pretend that we did. We mistrusted authority and took it in our own hands to invent creative solutions to overcome difficulties.

Most of us loved being back in school, loved returning to some semblance of normalcy. We had good teachers for the most part and an outstanding, varied academic curriculum. The school was a girls' school in a building without much heat, and we were crowded into small classrooms. We had a "brother" school nearby. Several times a year there were programs, dances, lectures, games, etc., where we could socialize with each other. I had zero interest in doing so at the time. Eleven- and twelve-year-old boys seemed painfully immature and boring to me. It took me a few years to change my mind on the subject.

I was eager to learn. I was curious by nature and wanted to discover as much about the world as I could, and preferably fast. First and foremost, I wanted to understand how what had happened to me, to us, could have happened. None of it made any sense. I was furious. I blamed the adults, my parents included. Why did they allow it? Why did they not fight back? Why did they not know any better? Lots of hard questions for an eleven-year-old. I did not know the answers then, and even now I am not sure. The one thing I thought I knew was that I did not intend to let it happen to me or mine again. I simply wouldn't allow it! So much for youthful arrogance.

School could be also disappointing and boring. For some reason I liked Latin—its concise, sensible structure and its condensed storytelling, amazing poetry, and wisdom nurtured my soul. We had to memorize much of the Aeneid, as well as Catullus, Sappho, Horace, Ovid, and much more. I still remember the beginning lines of the Aeneid: "Arma virumque cano..." ("I sing of arms and men..."). Young as I was, I thought I knew a lot about arms and men from personal experience. I devoured ancient Greco-Roman history. I was astounded at how little human behavior had changed in two thousand years. It made the immediate past somewhat more comprehensible, more bearable, and perhaps, in an odd way, more distant. Poetry transcended brutal reality. Words had the power to transform horror and ugliness into something beautiful and profound. Or so it seemed to me at the time.

For a precious four years we were encouraged to think for ourselves, discuss our ideas freely and value independence and free speech. Hungary had a long tradition of democratic values, at least in theory, if not practice.

So it was that I immersed myself in literature, music, and the fine arts with all the passion of a young, idealistic teenager. It was my therapy, my salvation, the only way I could heal.

I found theater and opera entirely fascinating. They immersed me in spectacle, nurtured all my senses, and penetrated my young adolescent soul with intense, often troubling emotions. I learned lessons about loyalty and integrity. Evil and destruction became more comprehensible and would be vanquished in the end. Love would eventually triumph through sacrifice and transcendence. Unrealistic perhaps, but a good counterpoint to the cynicism and despair threatening to engulf my heart and soul.

I had neither interest nor talent in athletics and could not hold a tune for the life of me. This was painful, because I loved music and had almost perfect pitch. I was fully aware whenever I hit a false note, but could not do anything about it. In the end, I was asked to lip-synch, but I was not excused from the school choir. I was duly embarrassed, but did not mind that much. I felt privileged to be able to listen to all the recently collected Hungarian folk tunes by Zoltan Kodaly and the exciting "new" music of Bela Bartok. We sang songs from the folk Opera *Háry János* and listened to the Hungarian Rhapsodies and songs of Franz Liszt and Brahms. I knew I could not sing or compose music, but I developed a life-long fascination with folk music, classical music and opera.

I thought I would become a writer. I started a diary. I wrote short stories for my literature classes. We all had to write papers. They were good, I was told. I became very cocky. One day I took a dare. I was particularly good at improvising and my classmates challenged me to read a nonexistent paper when I was next called on by the teacher, a story that was not written down or memorized, something

I had to make up on the spot. Our Lit teacher Miss L was small and mousy with a hunched back. She seemed very old to us. I think she must have been in her early fifties. She was kind and genuinely liked me. She believed in me. I liked her too, yet I was prepared to make a fool of her. I was convinced I could get away with it. I am not proud of this.

Me, happy, around 13 years old

Next day she called on me, sure enough. I stood up. She nodded for me to begin. A complete, ominous silence erupted in the classroom. I fervently wished I were somewhere else, anywhere else, but there was nowhere to go. I began to "read." I have no idea what my pseudo-paper was about. It could have been about Hungarian poetry or the plays of Shakespeare. It could have been anything, anything at all! All I remember is that I was holding a blank notebook, and I wished I was somewhere far away in space and time. On the moon perhaps. Everything went well for the first five minutes. Miss L was listening attentively, while the class was holding its breath in disbelief waiting for me to stumble. I carried on doggedly. As I hit my stride, my initial panic receded; the class, however, became increasingly restless, even agitated. Some started giggling, others began to fidget.

This was going too far. I kept on reading. I was about to finish. Miss L was no fool; she sensed something was wrong. While I was concentrating on my "reading," she left her seat behind her desk and reappeared next to me. She was looking over my shoulder at the notebook in my hand. The one that had nothing written on it. I was mortified and suddenly very ashamed, for Miss L was kind and gentle. She just told me to sit down and that it was a good try. Oh, and she took the empty notebook.

I was not punished, but I did learn a fundamental lesson. It had to do with respect and that it was very wrong to show off at the expense of others. Suddenly what seemed like derring-do became something cowardly and abusive, a no-win situation whether I succeeded or not. Especially if I succeeded. Thank you, Miss L, for teaching me a lesson I have never forgotten. Thank you for curbing my youthful arrogance. It needed a lot of curbing then and for a long time to come.

Picture of Class IIIA at Szilagyi Erzsebet "Gimnazium" ca. 1951.

7. My Brief Fling with Zionism and How I First Met Your Grandfather

Our new home was once again filled with people most evenings and weekends. Old and new friends came and went and were entertained with good food, good wine, and lively conversation. Father was more popular than ever and Mother was as always a gracious, brilliant hostess in spite of thinking that Father was too generous and kind to people who either "did not deserve it" or, worse, were dangerous to have around. I know this, because she often said so. In retrospect, she was probably right. It did not matter. It was Father's nature to be generous and to hold court, which he did.

We all thrived for a few years. I did well in school and made good friends. Lifelong friends, as it turned out. Agi, Marika, and I hung out every chance we had. The three of us were best friends and classmates throughout middle and high school. Others called us "The Three Musketeers." Yet we could not have been more different, and it is hard to see what glue held us together. Perhaps it was laughter. We stayed sane and survived amidst craziness by laughing in the face of disaster, defying the prophets of doom. We also shared a love of ideas, debate, books, theater, and folk and classical music.

I was the impulsive, idealistic rebel nerd with outlandish ideas who did not know how to keep her mouth shut and often got into trouble. Agi was the quiet, sensible one, a petite dark blonde with a lovely heart-shaped face, small blue eyes, tiny flower-petal lips, and a sweet soprano voice. Everybody loved Agi. We called her Macko ("little bear") despite her apparent physical fragility, maybe because she was slightly uncoordinated at times resulting perhaps from a severe case of encephalitis she had suffered the year before we met. She was determined, tough, and tenacious so the nickname fit her. In any case she accepted, even cherished it.

Marika was short, sturdy, and often "in your face." She was an excellent athlete and much in demand for team sports. Her abundant curly black hair vibrated with energy. You simply could not ignore her presence. Her voice was loud, penetrating, a powerful alto. This was necessary, as both her mother and her sister were deaf mutes. Gaby, her much-older sister, was beautiful and delicate and by necessity quiet, but her mother kept trying to speak, uttering guttural, mostly unintelligible sounds that only Marika could understand. They communicated mostly by sign language and lip reading, so Marika learned early on to speak loudly and distinctly. She had been their caretaker, interpreter, and guardian angel since childhood, their vital link to the world. There was no father in evidence. His exact fate remained a mystery sealed by the war. Like so many others, he disappeared without a trace. Marika never spoke of him. The three of them somehow survived in the ghetto and continued to live in a small, dark apartment on scant resources. Agi and I felt positively prosperous compared to Marika and she clearly considered us spoiled brats at times. Nevertheless, we adored her—her courage, her quick mind, her common sense, and her perseverance. It helped that she was a lot of fun, most of the time anyway.

One afternoon after school, Marika decided that we should go to the Hanhatz meeting and when Marika decided something, it usually happened. She was relentless, her enthusiasms hard to resist. It was easier just to give in. Besides, Agi and I were intrigued. Marika had recently joined the Hanhatz, aka Hanoir ha Zionim, a middle-of-the-road Zionist organization, and she absolutely loved it. This was during her first "Jewish" phase, in '47 or '48. We were thirteen and fourteen respectively. Marika was to have a number of subsequent enthusiasms, but we did not know that at the time.

"The people are fantastic. Everybody is so friendly and very smart and they are not particularly religious," she said when Agi and I objected on those grounds, albeit for different reasons.

Agi had been christened at birth, baptized, and was a practicing Roman Catholic in spite of the fact that the Nazis clearly thought otherwise. She and her family had to wear the yellow star in 1944 and were banished to the ghetto and persecuted, just like the rest of us. For the Nazis, if your grandparents were Jewish, so were you, vermin to be exterminated. You had to go. End of story.

Anyway, Agi had had an identity crisis the past couple of years, and not just for this reason. She had recently discovered that she was adopted. A gossipy neighbor had told her that her mom and dad were really her aunt and uncle and that she had three much-older birth brothers whom she knew as her cousins. I am not making this up! She checked the story and both sets of parents confessed under pressure. She was a late and unexpected addition to her birth family. Her aunt and uncle badly wanted a child and offered to adopt her. No harm done. After all, she stayed in the family and grew up as a cherished and protected (as much as possible) only child. Her cousins/brothers had fled to Israel by this time and she was open to finding out what Zionism was all about. Her parents remained staunch Catholics.

On the other hand, at age thirteen, I was vehemently against all organized religion, including Judaism. I saw religion as a major source of discrimination and intolerance based on my wartime experiences and reinforced by reading Bertrand Russell, who made a most convincing case on philosophical and historical grounds. I was probably also influenced by Marx's famous dictum that "religion is the opiate of the masses," which was one of the socialist concepts that resonated with me in those early post-war years.

Although Agi and I were mildly interested, we were wary of youth organizations. The Hitler Jugend and other fascist movements were fresh in our minds and our home-grown fledgling Communist youth organization "Pioneers" (Uttorok) did not sound particularly attractive, even at that early stage before the Communist takeover. Marika's accounts reassured us that Hanhatz was a relaxed, safe, stimulating, fun place to visit and one rainy day we did.

It turned out to be a very important day. Had we decided to go to see the movie Waterloo Bridge instead, or to our favorite cafe for some yummy chocolate pastry with whipped cream, my grandchildren would not have been born.

The Hanhatz headquarters occupied most of the second floor of a partially restored bombed-out building in Pest's VIIth district. We entered a dimly lit entrance hall (electricity was still very expensive and in short supply) and were greeted by a girl in her late teens named Miriam. Marika seemed to know her well. There was singing and laughter streaming from the depths of the apartment. Marika was eager to take us around. There were several young people gathered in one of the darkened rooms intently following the spotlight illuminating a small makeshift podium. At the podium was a tall, skinny seventeen-year-old with blazing red hair who was passionately reciting passages from *The Good Soldier Švejk*. His voice—a dynamic, masculine tenor—was strong, clear, and nuanced. He was both poetic and funny. I had never heard of or read Hašek, a Czech writer active in the early 20th century. The piece was an irreverent and hilarious satire on the absurd and devastating stupidity of WWI and of war in general, an early ancestor of *Catch 22.*

The crowd roared. I was hooked, smitten, and enchanted.

"Who is that? What is his name?" I asked Marika.

"We call him Piros (red) because of his hair. He is really, really smart. And nice," she added. There was awe in her voice. I did not fully realize it then, but Red's image in the spotlight became engraved in my soul. He did not know it, of course, but at that moment he came to represent for me the wonders and transcendence of art and poetry over the absurdities and limitations of our mundane existence. Tough expectations to live up to, and in the end, I was bound to be disappointed. For the next year or so I did not see much of Piros, although I became an enthusiastic member of Hanhatz. He was almost eighteen, four years older than I; we moved in different groups.

At that point I had no serious intention to move to Palestine (Israel did not yet exist), but Zionism made sense to me. Two years after the Holocaust, a secular Jewish State seemed like an insurance policy against further persecutions in the future. I was amazed to find out that efforts to establish one had begun in the late-19th and early-20th centuries. I fact-checked the information, another handy lesson from my past when "Fake Facts" were everywhere. I learned that Zionist organizations had helped the Resistance against the Nazis, hidden and rescued many Jews, and smuggled food to the ghetto, easing starvation. This information empowered me. I did not have to be ashamed anymore. Not every Jew went meekly to the slaughter following orders.

I imagined myself as Hannah Szenes, a young Jewish woman

who was active in the Resistance. She was both a poet and a fighter. She rescued countless people from deportation to Auschwitz. She was eventually betrayed by people she trusted and executed by the Nazis in 1944, towards the very end of the war. She became one of my early role models. Or so I imagined then. In reality, I have no inclination for violence, either then or now. For someone who often ended up in the midst of it, I truly hated conflict.

I saw Hanhatz as a liberal, but not ideology-driven, organization. Initially, it functioned as a club where I was always welcome, offering fun and good stimulating conversations with people who mostly cared about the same things I did. There was a general atmosphere of safety, acceptance, and mutual support, a good place to heal some of the wounds sustained during the war. I did not have to be on my guard for being born Jewish. I was not regarded as a second-class citizen. We had lively discussions on everything under the sun, including books, ideas, and politics. We read and recited poetry. We played games, listened to classical and folk music and danced the "Hora," a communal dance in which we held hands. It was the

Young Robi (Piros)

first—and for a long while the only—time in my life when I felt part of a community that didn't demand that I give up or betray my identity. It did not last long. Gradually I got sucked into an existence that was fundamentally alien to my nature.

In May 1948, Israel became an independent state. It was a joyous event. We marched barefoot over the Margit Bridge across the Danube, singing and rejoicing. Lots of young people of all religions and nationalities joined us in celebrating the miracle. After all the persecutions, we hadn't just survived, we had a country of our own. There would be peace now and everybody was going to live happily ever after. Or so we hoped. I can be forgiven; I did not know any better. Hope springs eternal, especially when you are very young.

After this, the pressure was on for us to emigrate. We were trained to live in a kibbutz. The kibbutzim were self-sufficient collective farming communities where individuals and families lived and "made the desert bloom." They still do.

Then, as now, most Arabs took a dim view of these new developments, so learning about self-defense became mandatory. We underwent training to survive in a hostile environment. We learned how to find shelter in the mountains and return to our home base. I still remember one of those exercises. I have no idea what possessed my parents to allow me to participate, but I recall being in the "wilderness" of the Buda hills with my group in the middle of the night. We had a leader with a compass and a mission to accomplish. I can't remember exactly what the mission was, except that it had something to do with reaching an assigned destination without being discovered by a rival group. This was the closest I have ever come to playing war games. I felt excited, adventurous, and a bit scared.

Then Piros showed up. I had not known he was around. He helped me climb the more challenging "mountains" and gave me useful tips on how to negotiate difficult terrain in the dark. He also offered me a hand when I needed it. I felt safe around him and his presence filled me with unexpected warmth during the chilly starlit night. We had to move around in silence, a shadow army trying to avoid detection. It was OK—we did not seem to need words, since we were enveloped in a cloak of mysterious closeness. I guess I fell in love that night, a kind of pure, spiritual love only a fourteen-year-old can experience, which seemed to evaporate in the light of day. It would surface many years later in unexpected ways. Instinctively, I never spoke to anyone about that night.

I did not see Piros after that. About six months later, I heard that Marika had pursued him and they were dating. Marika was very serious about it. I was happy for her, because she was my friend and it was the noble thing to do! Also, I was most definitely not ready to date.

About this time, it became clear we were being groomed for emigration. The Zionist leadership saw clearly what we didn't—the handwriting on the wall. Hungary's hijacking by the Stalinist regime was imminent. Time was running out. In spite of increasing doubts about emigrating, I agreed to join a haksara for three weeks in the summer when school was out. (Actually, I am not sure of the exact time span.) I felt brave and adventurous. The haksara was a kind of trial kibbutz, training us to survive in a harsh environment. We were a group of about sixteen boys and girls living in an old farmhouse in a "secret" location in the country. At not quite fourteen, I was by far the youngest, as usual. Everyone else was in their late teens.

Amenities were basic. We had running water and indoor plumbing, but no hot water. Air conditioning had not been invented yet. We had a wood-burning stove in the kitchen where, as cook, I had to prepare meals. I had been elected cook after an embarrassing failure as a farm hand. We were harvesting corn in our fields when both of my hands began to bleed profusely from the unaccustomed work. I felt profoundly humiliated as our leader, Dennis, a first-year medical student, bandaged them efficiently. I was in sickbay for the next several days.

I did not do much better as a cook. Breakfast was at sunup and I had lots of help, which was a good thing, as I was barely awake. I had to prepare lunches for everyone because they could not return from the fields until evening when they finished work. By that time, they were famished. I liked to eat even then, but I had no idea how to cook. I had never had to cook! There were no cookbooks around and no canned food. I did all right with some egg dishes and soup, but you can only feed farmhands so many pancakes and omelets. Everyone was very kind, but I knew I had to do something else soon. Dennis taught me how to cut up a chicken. He operated on the joints with surgical precision. To this day I think of him when I dismember a fowl.

Once I mastered roast chicken, I became ambitious and decided to make ravioli. Well, not really ravioli, the Hungarian version of it, called "monk's ear" for some reason. This involved making pasta dough from scratch, rolling it out, cutting it into rectangles and filling it with a cheese-and-egg mixture, then sealing the edges. They looked like miniature envelopes, not like monk's ears at all. It was labor intensive and a bit messy, but it was worth it. My friends deserved it. I was elated. All I had to do now was to drop the little envelopes in boiling salted water and that's when bad things started to happen. Instead of cooking, my monk's ears slowly disintegrated in the boiling water. I tried frantically to rescue some of them but wound up with a disgusting water-soaked mass of spongy dough. There was no time to prepare anything else. My friends arrived exhausted and very, very hungry. They were good-natured about it, but I had to admit to being a total failure both as a cook and as a farmhand.

Not long after this, my father appeared. He was on a rescue mission. He solemnly promised that we would all go to Israel together the next year, if only I came home now. I guess I was ready to be persuaded. I was not going to give up in defeat, but I was ready to go.

I missed home and I knew deep down that I was no good at roughing it, not yet. I simply did not have the skills and the stamina. Agi and Marika knew better; they never even attempted the haksara.

In the end, we didn't emigrate. Even if my father had meant it—and I am not sure now that he really did—by the next year it was too late. The borders were sealed by the Communist regime and we were trapped in our beautiful, tiny, oppressive country forever, as far as we could tell. Much later I learned that my friends had tried to cross the border a few months after I left, but they were captured and interned.

I returned to school in the fall, sobered and a little less crazy. For better or worse, this was home. I realized that I was not meant to be a farmer or a kibbutznik. I did not want to live in the desert, speak Hebrew, and fight Arabs. I did not want to leave my father and mother and Agi and Marika and the Buda hills.

Hungary may have been a bad, abusive parent at times, but she was my parent, my culture, my language. Sure, I was angry with her, but I was only fourteen and not ready to abandon her, to leave my home. I did eventually, but not before I had suffered a lot more abuse.

8. Siofok: The Exile

By the time I was sixteen years old, the next vicious storm of tyranny had caught up with us once again. The coalition government was dissolved and the Hungarian Communist Party took over the Government. This was during the most frightening period of Stalin's reign, personified in Hungary by Mátyás Rákosi's oppressive Communist regime. Rakosi was a Hungarian, the fourth of 13 children. He was trained in Moscow after WWI. He became a favorite of Stalin's before becoming the all powerful Prime Minister of Hungary in 1949. His reign of terror lasted for 10 years.

In our house, free speech was the norm. This wasn't altogether smart as it turned out. Little by little, "friends" started disappearing: some because Father became increasingly and vocally politically incorrect, others because they were caught up in the political infighting and found themselves on the wrong side.

I particularly remember Istvan, one of Father's admirers and a frequent visitor at the house. He was tall, dark, and handsome, a dashing young officer. I think I had a crush on him, because I tried to hang around whenever he was there. I admired his passion for rebuilding the country and establishing a just social order. He was a rising leader in the Communist party, full of idealism and dead set on saving the country from both the right-wing neo-fascists and the emerging extreme Stalinist factions. One day he disappeared. Nobody knew his whereabouts until quite a few months later when he was tried for treason against The People's Republic. It was a mock trial. He was found guilty and executed mostly because he belonged to the inner circle of László Rajk, the Interior Minister and Head of Homeland Security. Rakosi was engaged in a power struggle with Rajk and won. Istvan was one of the many victims.

This was only the beginning of things to come. Father, a Social Democrat of national stature (President of the National Association of Dental Laboratories and Technicians, among other things) became persona non grata. He somehow managed to escape arrest, but his highly successful and innovative laboratory was taken over by the Government. In addition, he was forbidden to practice in Budapest. My beloved home was confiscated—or as the Communists preferred to call it, "bought"—for a nominal sum and assigned to a Communist couple in good standing. My parents were ordered to move to Siofok, a small resort town on Lake Balaton. Father got an official document stating that there was a dentist shortage in Siofok and it was his duty to serve the people there. We had only a few weeks to make the transition.

This was exile.

There were certainly worse places than Siofok—it wasn't the Gulag by a long shot. It was beautiful in summer but dreary and desolate the rest of the year. In those days, Siofok had no decent schools, colleges, or cultural organizations. It had a small public library, and that was about it. I was about to enter my junior year in high school and it was decided that I should stay in Budapest to graduate and hopefully transition to University.

Apart from the logistics and general hassle of moving and leaving behind family and friends, the biggest problem for my parents became the chimney sweep. Or rather the family of the chimney sweep. The small one-family home allocated by the Government for Father and Mother as a residence and dental practice was by no means empty when they got there. It contained the chimney sweep, his wife, and his grown daughter. This was a surprise both to my parents and the chimney sweep. It was not a pleasant surprise. The chimney sweep was a nice guy who was rarely home. When he was around, he was usually covered in soot. I liked his daughter, who was pretty and in her early twenties and attracted a constant stream of young male visitors.

The real problem was Vilma, aka Mrs. Chimney Sweep. She was in her late fifties, older than my mom, and she was tough, combative, and vulgar. In our supposedly classless society, disapproval and distrust of "fancy" city folks was rampant. Probably vice versa. In addition, we were Jewish, which was not a good thing in the Hungarian countryside in 1949, or perhaps even today. Vilma's standards of cleanliness were questionable at best. She took control of the kitchen and the only bathroom as well as two bedrooms on the other side of the bungalow. In Hungarian folklore, chimney sweeps were supposed to bring luck, but we did not feel lucky at all! It was not a good situation.

My mother had to improvise a kitchen in the entry hall using a butane gas burner and a sink with a pipe connected to the "surgery" that took up the front of the house. She not only cooked fantastic meals there, but also produced the best, most beautiful cakes and pastry you can imagine. I have no idea how she managed it, but she was a gifted chef. When Mother was not cooking and cleaning up, she functioned as the dental assistant for my father. She was well-trained as she had done this for many years in their previous lives in Budapest.

There was a toilet in my parents' part of the house, but taking a bath became a major problem. This gave Mrs. Chimney Sweep immense power to blackmail. She would grant magnanimous access in return for fresh fried chicken, homemade potato chips, and cookies and cakes. These things were rare and expensive in those days, not to mention labor intensive in our minimalist kitchen. Vilma was capricious. She would withdraw bath access without much warning, depending on her mood. Even when all went well, the bathroom wasn't all that clean and we had to spend much of our precious time there scrubbing the tub.

No one had dishwashers, food processors, or electronic gadgets. Families sometimes had iceboxes to keep perishables. The iceman came once a week and we purchased a large chunk of ice—the size of a small side table—to fit the ice compartment. There was a drain at the bottom that had to be emptied from time to time. Even so, when we bought live fish from the fishermen at the market, we had to keep it in a big tub until it was time to cook it. I remember making uneasy acquaintance with giant keszeg, fogas, and ponty (delicious carp and pike unique to the region). Mother had to cook on the small makeshift stove using firewood. There were no kitchen cabinets. She worked in the entry hall, which was drafty and cold in the winter and suffocatingly hot in the summer. There was no privacy, with strangers constantly coming and going.

In the end, Father resolved the bathroom issue by providing dental care to the local innkeeper and his wife. Both Aranka and Gyozo were short and obese, Aranka morbidly so. They were in their fifties, uneducated but smart, a power to reckon with in the community. They probably got ahead by cooperating with the Communist government, but their heart was not in it. Mostly they used their influence to help people. Like most in those days, they did what they had to do to survive. Except for my father, who did not compromise. His gift was to influence people and enlist their support. He was charismatic. The fact that he could almost always stop a toothache when no one else could helped. Aranka and Gyozo were happy to provide a weekly bath for my family in exchange for dental care. When I was home in the summer, I was part of the deal and became the unwilling object of Aranka's affection. She never had any children.

I was displaced once again, but I was lucky and escaped exile. I lost my home, but I was allowed to stay in school. I stayed in Budapest and lived with Uncle Rezso and Aunt Jeanette for a while. It wasn't a good idea and it did not last very long. They didn't have children of their own, and Jeanette was ill-prepared to put up with an active, strong-minded teenager. Although I was reasonably well-behaved, I was talkative, bursting with energy, sloppy, and used to getting a lot of attention. Jeanette was controlling, a complainer who generally did not like anybody very much, except for Uncle Rezso. On second thought, she liked to complain about him too.

Nobody was happy. After about six months it was time to make a change. As much as I loved Juci and Zoli, it seemed wise to avoid inserting myself into another hitherto childless couple's life. I knew they were there if I needed them and I would be invited for dinner on the weekends, but I wanted to be independent. Father eventually understood and arranged to rent a small room for me in the home of a friend of a friend, with the understanding that they would look out for me.

Housing wasn't my biggest problem, however. It became harder and harder to navigate school. It may be difficult to believe now, but informers were everywhere. There was a great deal of pressure on the students to join the Young Communist Organizations and report on the rest of us. Not everyone did this, but every class had at least one misguided or opportunistic soul. Ours was Olga. We could not be sure, but there was a lot of circumstantial evidence otherwise inexplicable. Sixty years later when I saw her at our school reunion in Budapest, she still insisted that she did not report on us. By then she had left the Communist party, disillusioned and repentant of her youthful mistakes. But that's another story.

In any case, I was increasingly harassed by the powers-that-be. The school authorities bombarded me with questions: Why did I not participate in the First of May parade (a very important celebration for the Communists, a national holiday)? Sickness was not a good excuse. Why did I not join the Young Communists? Why did I read decadent and subversive bourgeois literature such as *The Magic Mountain* by Thomas Mann?

At one point I was summoned before a panel of teachers and Party dignitaries in the principal's office. This was a serious matter that could possibly have resulted in disciplinary measures, including expulsion. My crime? Several things had come to their attention. I participated in a "ring" that listened to long-playing records of Wagner operas and other "Nazi" music. My friends and I read Nietzsche and Sartre and other existential philosophers. We read "decadent" Western literature that did not hold to Marxist-Leninist doctrine. I had made disparaging remarks about the doctrines of "socialist realism," the prevailing standard of Communist art theory. They went on and on.

In the end I was excused with a warning. Clearly the panel had been instructed by the Party to discipline me, but their hearts were not in it. Most likely they read the same books and listened to the same music I did. From then on, I understood that I needed to keep my interests and opinions under cover. I needed to be careful who I talked to or shared my activities with. To survive, I had to stay on high alert much, if not most, of the time. This went against my nature and was difficult for me to maintain.

Not everything was bleak, though. I increasingly found my consolation in poetry, literature, and the theater. Hungarian poets and writers had a long tradition of fighting for freedom of expression and democracy. Hungarian translations of the great Western classics as well as the works of contemporary artists were available in used bookstores, if you knew where to look. It also helped that I could read English and French. Paradoxically, sanctioned Russian literature was also an inspiration for political and ideological dissent. The observations and passion of Tolstoy, Chekov, Dostoyevsky, and even Mayakovsky were as damning of the totalitarianism of the Soviet regime as they were of their own historical realities.

I was fortunate to have good friends, kindred spirits to hang out with, to confide in. I was immersed in learning, discovering a wondrous world of ideas and inspiration. I fell in love with theater. I no longer wanted to be a writer. I wanted to put on plays, to dissect and direct them. To understand human motivation and behavior. To understand what made people do what they did. Why did they say one thing and do something completely different? How did they become evil and destructive? All that and more was hidden in the plays, and actors and directors made it come to life. I was too self-conscious to act, but I could analyze and direct. I was certain of that. So one day in my junior year, I applied to the Academy of Drama and Theater in Budapest, a kind of Hungarian Juilliard. It was perhaps the most competitive university in the country, the only one of its kind. It was an insane thing to do, but I was in love. In love with the theater. The chances of being selected were infinitesimal. I was a very good student, true, but I was politically suspect. Still, I applied and was called in for an audition. After an extended and grueling selection process, to my enormous surprise and delight, I was accepted.

Naturally, it did not last. Less than a year later, I managed to get not only expelled but also barred from entering any other university in the country. How did I do it? It was not difficult. I spoke my mind freely. Among other things, I said that Comrade Zhdanov's principles of socialist realism were laughable and at odds with common sense and all the known principles of aesthetics. This was not a smart thing to do. I was branded "a bourgeois, avant-garde enemy of the people." I was actually surprised. I believed in free speech, social justice, and everyone contributing to the common good according to their best abilities and receiving according their needs. These were the Marxist principles taught in school. I learned the hard way that people, especially governments, did not always practice what they preached and Stalinism was a sort of nihilism using ideas as tools of deception, exploitation, and tyranny. This was the playbook written to advance Soviet imperialism. Until then—and against all evidence to the contrary—I thought I was free. I should have known better.

After my expulsion from the Academy, my whole world collapsed—it was wiped out, erased, eradicated. I fled to Siofok to recover under the protective love and care of my parents. I went into hibernation. I slept most of the day, rarely emerging from my room, and then only under duress to eat a bite or two or take a walk by Lake Balaton. I hardly spoke to anyone, but I wrote profusely, if not too coherently, in my diary. This probably saved my sanity. This, and my parents' gentle love and wisdom in letting me mourn at my own pace.

This went on for several weeks. Time was disintegrating, as was so much else in my life. And then it all stopped, as abruptly as it began. I emerged from my cave. I sat and read in the sun in the garden for long hours like an invalid recuperating from a long illness. The wisdom of the written word and the rhythm of poetry filled my soul with joy and hope. I listened to music, mostly classical. The passionate struggles of Beethoven dwarfed my problems and gave me strength; the playful wisdom of Mozart lifted my spirit. I moved from the garden to the beach and read some more in the sun. When I could read no more, I watched the movements of the light skimming the waves and the shimmering leaves of the trees weaving patterns in the breeze, and it was all good. My soul filled with awe. I loved the sky, the moon, and the stars, and my spirits lifted. I was ready to go back and fight. I was going to find a way to build a good life and enjoy the process no matter how rough the road.

Since I was still young, gifted, and judged harmless, the powers-that-be decided there was hope for me yet. I was ordered to work in a factory to "redeem" myself. At eighteen, in one fell swoop, I was transformed from a promising student of an elite University to a novice member of "The Proletariat" (a state of distinction in the Stalinist period). In my case, this meant working in a factory manufacturing cocoa powder and chocolates. It could have been worse. We were assigned positions on competing production teams. Each week a winning team was declared based on productivity. By the following week, the winning performance was declared the new performance standard. And so on, ad infinitum. They called this the Stakhanov system. Wages were based on how closely you approximated the winning team's productivity. The wages were not living wages, but we were reminded that we "owned" the factory. To this day I have no idea what this meant. It became abundantly clear, however, even for me, that we were being exploited big time.

I spent eight to ten hours a day on my feet trying to keep up with the assembly line, wearing coarse, ill-fitting shoes and inhaling the fake cocoa powder we packaged for breakfast drinks. It saturated my pores and all other available orifices—my ears, nose, eyes, and throat. I worked as fast as I could, and sometimes faster. When I got

Soaking up the sun and surf in a small boat
on Lake Balaton

home after an hour-and-a-half commute on crowded public transportation, my first move was to soak in a tub that was barely big enough to sit in. I poured in lukewarm water warmed on a gas range in an effort to remove as much of the ubiquitous stuff as possible. For years afterwards, the smell of cheap chocolate nauseated me.

Eventually I was transferred to another factory. Escaping from cocoa, I was now immersed in detergents. We produced and packaged soaps of all sorts. Persil was the big name for getting clothes clean. It had bleach in it. Not good to inhale. We wore kerchiefs to cover our hair, but we had no masks. I was one of the youngest there and some of the workers were protective of me. They taught me patience, perseverance, and self-confidence through hard physical work. They had to struggle, using their last ounces of strength to keep their heads above water, to feed and house their families and themselves. Eventually I stopped seeing myself as some sort of wimpy female Hercules who had to undergo impossible trials for some unnamed, unknown transgression. In my youthful grandiosity, I imagined that hostile gods were trying hard to dampen my spirits and teach me humility. It began to dawn on me that I was merely one of many lost souls trying to survive and find a measure of happiness and meaning in life. I was making some progress, but I still had a very long way to go. It didn't help that I still thought that humility was somewhat overrated. In any case, I was determined not to give up.

Looking back, the worst thing was my profound sense of isolation. I was tolerated, even accepted, but I didn't exactly fit in at the factory. My life had taken a turn that was almost incomprehensible to my old friends and companions. Not surprisingly, they seemed to slowly disappear. Agi was in medical school, studying very hard and building a life with her future husband and fellow student Laci. Marika was entering her Communist phase and we ceased to have anything in common. My friends from the Academy, after an initial furtive declaration of sadness and empathy, avoided me, or I avoided them, or perhaps both. Our lives took drastically different turns and I knew that association with me in the prevailing political atmosphere was a liability to them. It was a rough, but mercifully brief, phase in my life.

One day after I had been at the factory for eight months or so, the office had a staff shortage over the holidays and I was "elevated" temporarily to join them because I knew how to spell and write and had basic skills in arithmetic. I accepted with glee. First, I did not have to get up at 4 a.m.; the office did not open until 8 a.m. Secondly, the administrative staff was an island of sanity not entirely controlled by the Party. They played the game, but most of them were well-educated and aware of the insanity and hypocrisy of the system. They were professionals who knew what they were doing. The factory was actually profitable for the Party and had some leeway from outside control. They "adopted" me, as you would a stray cat. I tried to do my best to repay their kindness. I got a much better education there on how the world really worked than I could have gotten at University.

Several months later, with the front office's recommendation, I got an administrative job at the Ministry of Export-Import due to my knowledge of English, German, and some Russian and French. This was a big change. I got to work civilized hours in downtown Pest, away from the factory, and the pay was better—much, much better. Not great, but at least I made a living wage. The Communist regime did what everyone else did and what they said they never would; white-collar workers were paid better than factory workers, and bureaucrats (Party Leadership) were paid better still. By then, I was not surprised.

The first thing I did with my larger paycheck was to order a pair of shoes that actually fit. They were soft, comfortable burgundy loafers. I soon discovered that this was not a wise thing to do. It got me into Big Trouble. I often got into Big Trouble in those days. Communists frowned on custom-made shoes, or custom-made anything. Never mind that there wasn't anything else. This was explained to me by a kind, fatherly big boss who had once been a Social Democrat but had somehow managed to avoid the Purge. I did not inquire how; it was probably because his parents were laborers and he knew the right people.

"Keep a low profile," he said. "Black shoes are OK, but burgundy attracts attention. And you have narrow feet, so you look too bourgeois, too elegant. Get something wide and clunky. And keep your mouth shut. It won't do to look too happy."

He was quite right. It was then I finally, if somewhat belatedly, realized that I was living in a "Country of Lies" and that things wouldn't get any better.

9. Falling in Love

I was now the ripe age of almost eighteen, feeling about one hundred eighteen—world weary, worn out, disappointed, and disempowered. I was not ungrateful for surviving the Nazis and the bombs and the fighting, but to what end had I survived? Communism not only made the present difficult, it took away my future. Now I think my adolescent despair may have been exaggerated. True, I was shut out of academia and my passion for the theater and the arts seemed destined to die of starvation, but I had a decent salaried job with the government and opportunities for promotion. I liked my coworkers and had good friends. My parents were getting by—even settling down—in Siofok and I was still the apple of their eye.

Why was I at such loose ends? The short answer was: there was something rigid and uncompromising in my nature. I was flexible enough in everyday living—where I lived, how often I moved, how much money I had. Details of everyday living did not trouble me unduly. Part of me actually enjoyed rolling with the punches. It was different when it came to fundamental existential issues, such as the recognition that I was living in a vast prison where I could be rewarded for "good behavior" which, to me, meant behaving unethically or, more likely, that I could be punished at any time for dissent or disobedience for living by my principles.

I craved freedom. I had never been free. I had only dreamt about it and read about it. I did not want to be controlled by the system. I wanted to be able to say what I thought. I wanted open debate, a free exchange of ideas. I wanted to read the books I wanted to read, not what the Party wanted me to read. I wanted to travel where I liked and live where I liked, not to be confined to a small country the size of Delaware, however interesting!

First and foremost, I was tired of being fed lies. Lies about being free, when we were not, of equality, when there was none, of prosperity, when food was scarce and there were long lines for bread and meat and fresh fruit at the stores and many were starving because the economy was being destroyed by Stalinist dogma. I was tired of malice and stupidity pervading every aspect of our lives. I was tired of the perpetual vigilance required to survive. Furthermore, I was not alone feeling these things and thinking these things. I was angry and disappointed with the passion only a young person can have. Part of me despaired of the future. I suspect I was very close to giving up, drowning in despair.

At this point, Fate intervened. I was about to learn another important lesson about relationships, about love…

One dark and rainy fall afternoon I was riding the crowded tram on my way home from work when a dark, handsome young man in his early twenties began waving at me frantically from the other end of the train. His curly hair and huge brown eyes with long lashes would have been the pride and joy of any teenage girl or young woman. He soon made his way to where I was standing, not an easy feat to accomplish. At this point my bewilderment gave way to reluctant recognition. It was Duckie. He was a buddy of Piros. I had last seen him three or four years before, and he seemed to have changed a lot. Perhaps for the better? He seemed less obnoxious and full of himself. He was still very handsome. Duckie used to hang out with Piros (whose real name was Robi) at Hanhatz, the now defunct and outlawed Zionist youth organization. His real name was Charlie, but he was known by the nickname Duckie for reasons unknown. I think he loved swimming and sailing—perhaps that explains it.

When Duckie flagged me down, I was not too enthusiastic. Back when I was thirteen, he had not paid any attention to me, but now that I was almost eighteen, he embraced me like a long-lost friend. "You look beautiful! We have to get together," he insisted.

It turned out that he was still in touch with Robi and he insisted on arranging a kind of reunion that included Robi, Marika, Agi, and us. There was no time for me to object or ask questions; the tram was crowded as usual and I had to get off at the next stop. I felt ambushed, but there was no reason to be unkind or rude, I told myself, so I agreed. It turned out that Marika was out of town and could not be reached. I suspected that Duckie thought I was going to be his date and this troubled me. "Well, this is not a dating situation, more like a reunion of old friends," I thought. The truth was, I was intrigued by the prospect of seeing Piros again.

Why wasn't I interested in Duckie? I remembered him as obnoxious, conceited, self-centered, and very much in love with himself. He used to consider himself a playboy. Even if he wasn't, I was uninterested and inexperienced with dating. Men did pay attention to me, and I learned to take that for granted. I had male friends, but that's all they were—friends. My mind was in the clouds and my sexuality was buried deep under layers of lofty ideas as well as insecurities and mistrust. So why did I give Duckie my phone number? Good question. For one thing, Duckie could be very persuasive, not to say pushy. For another, I was reluctant to be rude for no apparent reason. Finally, finding out what had happened to everyone was tempting. The "everyone" I was most interested finding out about was Piros.

So when Duckie called with the arrangements for our get together, Agi and I accepted. Marika was on one of her out-of-town projects and could not come. I can't remember where we met. It might have been at Café Gerbeaud, on Vörösmarty Square, a sumptuous Viennese-style coffeehouse with gleaming chandeliers, gilded easy chairs, and delicately carved tables, which served heavenly, world-famous pastries, and other delicacies. An incongruous place in the midst of Communist austerity.

As far as I was concerned we could have been on the moon or somewhere in outer space among the stars. All I remember is this amazing feeling of connection, of being engulfed in the encounter with the Other. It was the end of isolation, of separateness, of not belonging. It was love. Piros and I had eyes and ears only for each other.

Piros said he was going to call me and we would go out together and that was that. Duckie called me first. He said he was disappointed about how things went, but he understood.

"These things happen. You and Piros simply clicked," he said.

I thought this was the understatement of the year, but thanked him for being understanding.

"Nevertheless, don't be surprised if you don't hear from Piros," he added. "He has been in an intense, stormy relationship for quite some time. It is not good for him, but so far he has been unable to extricate himself."

Duckie's opinion was that this "femme fatale" had some kind of emotional stranglehold on Piros and he did not think this would change in the near future.

"I am here for you," he said encouragingly, clearly not minding being second choice.

I was surprised and flattered, since Duckie had a very high opinion of himself in general and especially where women were concerned. In any case he was mistaken. Piros did call, and very soon. I remember eyeing the telephone every few minutes when I was home. I knew it was stupid and it felt demeaning, but I could not help myself. I can still picture this big black phone squatting on a table in the hall like some nasty toad. It was the old-fashioned dial kind. The numbers were black on a dazzling white background. It practically shouted at me to place a call. I did not. I did not want to be the pursuer. I felt very strongly that he had to come to me. For us to be happy, he had to want to take the initiative. And he did.

The call was anything but private. The phone sat in the hall. It had a long cord, but not long enough. People were listening. We set up a date at the nearby coffeehouse for the next day. It was wonderful. He was already there when I arrived. Waiting. We passionately discussed philosophy, politics, poetry, literature, the fate of the world, and similar lofty things for hours.

Later we went to concerts and the theater. We went dancing. He was an excellent dancer. Many Hungarian men were. I loved it. We were good together; we naturally synchronized our movements. We were particularly spectacular at dancing the tango. My father had taught me when I was thirteen or fourteen. He would put on a scratchy long-playing record of "La Cumparsita" and show me how to sidestep and turn and twirl. I put that knowledge to good use dancing with Piros. He was quite impressed.

I had had fun before with boyfriends while I was still in my asexual period simply enjoying the attention and companionship of my friends. I was probably quite naïve, ignoring bids for increased emotional involvement. At seventeen or eighteen, I had many other things on my mind. I did not want to be touched by anyone who did not touch my soul. I was very old fashioned that way, if not in anything else. I don't know why. Sexual mores in post-war Hungary, like today, were modern and uninhibited. The Communists believed in "free love" and the equality of women, theoretically at least.

In any case, meeting Piros changed all that. But not right away. I told him that I knew about his ongoing relationship and I did not wish to interfere with it. It was a lie, of course, and I knew it as soon as I said it! I wanted to be noble, but I hoped that he would throw everything and everyone to the wind for me because I was his "true love." I must have read too many 19th-century romantic novels and poetry. Amazingly, it turned out that he actually did just that! He said that his relationship with V had been on and off for quite a while, that she kept seeing other people, but when he wanted out, she would pursue him and he would succumb. Now he said, "I want to see only you." I believed him, and it turned out to be true. I felt the same way, but I had a less complicated life. I did not know enough to worry about forming a relationship on the rebound. This was a good thing, since it never became a problem. There were other things I should have worried about, perhaps, such as my total lack of experience in dating, but I am not sure it would have made any difference. I had found my soul mate, my true love, and it was mutual.

I became immersed in this wonderful new world of intimacy, of loving unconditionally and being loved and cherished uncon- ditionally in return. Life was illuminated by love. Everything else seemed secondary. My expulsion from higher education, the loss of any academic or creative future or meaningful career, even, at least temporarily, my despair over my lack of freedom and living in a toxic environment –all of this diminished and became part of the background noise, dwarfed by our finding each other. Amazing thing, love. Young love especially.

10. Courtship

By the time I met Robi again, my life circumstances had improved considerably. I was working at Ministry Headquarters in a decent, if not overly exciting, job managing export-import transactions. I had rejoined the "middle class." I was among decent, well-educated people who were friendly and seemed to accept me for the most part. I had made new friends, and for the first time in my life I could support myself independently. I felt self-confident and pretty much grown up. I was almost nineteen.

In Hungary in the 1950s, work days were long and the work week included at least half days on Saturdays. All women were expected to work; the regime wouldn't tolerate stay-at-home mothers. Grandparents, if they were alive, were expected to help with child care and some cooking. Domestic help was not allowed. This meant that the women had to take care of cleaning, washing, marketing, children, and everything else in the evenings after work and during the truncated weekends. Men were not expected to help at home, but they often had to take extra part time jobs to make ends meet. We all had to attend Communist indoctrination meetings in the mornings and sometimes after work, whether or not we were Party members. I was not.

I knew that I had it relatively easy, even though I had to fend for myself, because I did not yet have a family to take care of. I also had my uncles to turn to in an emergency, and they invited me for wonderful meals on weekends. Robi worked long hours, but his job gave him a lot more flexibility than mine, because he did not have to punch a time card. He supported his mother and grandmother, who lived in the same household and took care of all household chores. They coddled their only remaining son.

Perhaps we had more opportunities than most couples to see each other every day after work and on weekends, and we talked on the phone when we were not together. But it still required a great deal of effort and planning. Not that we complained! When we were together, we were happy. We laughed about the absurdities of life around us and pretended to resolve all the pressing problems of the day. After finding remedies for all the world's ills, we would hug and make love on the rare occasions when we found a place to be alone.

We went to wonderful outdoor restaurants in the summer, eating fresh pike and carp caught in the Danube. There would be live music by a gypsy orchestra and we would dance until we were out of breath, which was a pretty long time. The virtuoso violinist, usually the band leader, would often come up and serenade me with love songs ordered and paid for by Robi. This was an accepted form of courtship in those days in Hungary. I laughed and was embarrassed by all this romantic stuff, of course, but I enjoyed it greatly nevertheless. We would wander around Castle Hill in Buda and stop in a small hidden wine bar in an ancient, unrestored, bombed-out building in the shadow of the great gothic cathedral of St. Matthias (Matyas). There we would drink strong espresso chased by rare imported cognac, listening to the gifted pianist play forbidden jazz and sing in his wonderful raspy voice.

In quiet, thoughtful moods, we walked the banks of the Danube at sunset, holding hands and reciting poetry. We sat on the lower banks of the river at twilight and listened to the chatter of the waves on the surface and the silence of the depth of the river, as my favorite poet, Attila József, described:

> I sat there on the quayside by the landing,
> a melon rind was drifting on the flow.
> I delved into my fate, just understanding:
> the surface chatters, while it's calm below.
>
> "By the Danube," translation by
> Peter Zollman, lines 1-4

We went to the opera and afterwards Robi would sing the tenor arias, to my delight. He was a great *Trovatore* (a favorite opera by Verdi). We went to the theater and debated the merits and flaws of the play, the interpretation, and the performance. We had very strong opinions about these things and our debates were often heated. Theater was a very important part of Hungarian culture and often provided coded messages/metaphors regarding the oppressive political system. It was, and to some extent still is, truly democratic, affordable to all but the most destitute. We also had endless discussions about the books we read and the ideas we shared. Our idealism was boundless, or at least mine was. Robi tended to be more realistic.

We walked for hours and hours all over town and be-

Robi posing on top of Mount Gellert at the Citadel in Buda

yond, because we liked to be in motion. Our gaits, our whole bodies, were in sync with each other. This was not easy, as Robi was over six feet tall and I was a bit under five foot four. Nevertheless, we learned to adjust our strides to each other. Holding hands helped. We loved and admired the endless, constantly shifting beauty of both cities. Walking was a good way for us to be together and alone. This became a pattern that persisted for much of our lives. We would walk to grab precious moments of privacy from Robi's mother and grandmother, who were always quite intrusive, like most parents in those days. Later, we used the walking method when we wanted to get away from our children.

We both worked during the day. Robi was an Assistant Professor on the Faculty of Civil Engineering at the Műegyetem (University of Technology and Economics) in Budapest. It was—and still is—the Hungarian equivalent of MIT, the most significant university of its kind in Hungary and well-respected throughout Europe. Founded in 1782, it is considered the world's oldest Institute of Technology with university rank and structure. It was the first institute in Europe to train engineers at the university level.

I still have no idea how he managed to achieve his position without joining the Communist Party. Perhaps because he was, and continued to be, something of a structural design prodigy, then and now a rare commodity. He had a natural instinct for and solid knowledge of how to design and restore bridges that actually worked and did not fall down. Building bridges was a crucial growth industry in post-war Hungary. The retreating Nazi army blew up everything they could, including most of the bridges in the country, in their futile effort to slow down the Russian advance. In 1950, most of the rebuilding of the infrastructure was yet to be done.

Robi had the good fortune to be mentored and advanced by the

most influential professor in his field in Academia. He was then—
and for the rest of his long life—creative, a hard worker, and a per-
fectionist. Robi also had excellent survival instincts. He was naturally apolitical and knew when to keep his mouth shut, a crucial
attribute I did not master until much later in my life and even then,
not very well.

I knew nothing about all this when we met. I knew next to nothing about engineering and very little about architecture beyond what
you get studying art history of various periods. I found out about his
interests, abilities, and successes gradually and in increments. Some
of it I learned from his family and friends. I saw firsthand, however,
the practical help he dispensed lavishly. He could fix anything. He
could build things. He could find his way in the dark in the middle
of a mountain path—he never got lost. He could do many things I
could not do myself.

I wanted to love and nurture him, for he had had many losses.
His father died at a young age—around fifty—during the war years
of a heart attack induced by the stress of the times. His adored older
brother died in a concentration camp at age seventeen. Robi himself
had barely survived the hardships of the war in the ghetto in Budapest. He never talked about how. Now, as the only surviving male in
his family, he was the sole support for his mother and grandmother.
At twenty-three, he took this responsibility very seriously. This pattern persisted all through his life.

By some unspoken mutual agreement, we kept our relationship
relatively private, especially from our parents. At that point we were
pretty selfish. We did not want to share each other with anyone. We
did not want to "discuss our relationship" and we did not want to
answer any questions.

One summer evening after darkness had fallen, we were saying our goodbyes (which tended to be lengthy and delicious) in the shadows by the entrance of the apartment house where I lived, when my mother suddenly appeared. This was unexpected. She lived in

Robi in a relaxed mood.

Siofok with my father, several hours' train ride away. They did not own a car and they seldom visited. Apparently, my mother had been seized by an irresistible urge to feed and nourish me. She was carrying a gallon-sized jar of chicken soup, because that's what Jewish mothers do. Especially Hungarian Jewish mothers. Of course, she might also have been a bit curious. My parents knew I was seeing someone and must have suspected that I was in love, although I had not said so. So there was Mother, finding her one and only daughter in the arms of a stranger in the middle of the night!

It was an awkward situation, at least briefly. Fortunately, both Mother and Robi rose to the occasion. Sheltered only by the arches of the doorway, in the middle of the night, they politely expressed their mutual pleasure at meeting, after which Robi executed a rapid but dignified departure, which my Mother accepted graciously, still clutching her jar of chicken soup. Once we got upstairs, I had a lot of explaining to do. Why had I not told them about Robi? Who was he, and how did we meet? When? Where? There were lots of questions and we stayed up late talking. I could tell that Mother rather liked him. Fortunately, this turned out to be mutual. Robi and my parents always got on very well and genuinely enjoyed each other's company.

Now that the cat was out of the bag, as it were, we absolutely had to visit my parents in Siofok. My father wanted to meet Robi and Father was not particularly mobile. It was hard for him to negotiate the railroad. Old-fashioned steam locomotives were still operating in Hungary in those days, and they had steep narrow steps with huge gaps between them and the platform. They were a challenge for a tall, heavy-set, elderly man with a bum leg and emphysema.

Our first joint visit went well, as did subsequent visits. The weather was good and beautiful Lake Balaton was at its seductive best. We swam during the day until we were exhausted, raced each other to the shore, and collapsed on the hot sand. We rubbed each other's backs and shoulders and chests with bergamot, a special oil to promote tanning without sunburn. We both had very fair skin and were prone to turn red as boiled crabs if we were not careful. Most of the time we were alone on the beach. Siofok in those days was not the slick, cosmopolitan resort it is now. Off-season and during the week, it was quiet and peaceful and very private. It was a wonderful, sheltered place.

My little black dog Maszat often tagged along. She was a miniature puli, the Hungarian version of a toy poodle, smart and funny and beautiful—an absolute delight. Mother and I would dress her up in a skirt and a top with a headscarf and she thought it was great fun. I have an old picture of Maszat on her hind legs between Mother and me, each of us holding her by one of her front paws like you would a toddler. She was silly cute, but Robi and I didn't always want her around. We would try to sneak out unobserved, but she always found us. Maszat would not let us cuddle. She had an uncanny ability to get between us. She was not content to sit by my side, or even on my lap.

She did not want to play favorites. She would squeeze her little body between us as we sat blissfully on the beach, enjoying the rhythmic sounds of the waves crashing, the ever-changing light on and above the water, the shifting shapes of clouds, the looming mountain ranges on the other side of the lake. There we sat communing with nature, brimming with love, Robi and me and this fuzzy little black dog! This was heaven!

Mother always outdid herself when we were there. In addition to Father and me, now she had Robi to feed and spoil. Robi loved it. He loved the attention, the cooking, the cakes, and her affectionate spirit. He loved his own mother too, but her cooking was pretty dismal and she was not particularly effusive. Also, Mother would never dream of yelling at Robi as she did at Father or me. As far as she was concerned, Robi walked on water. He could do no wrong. Father's approval of Robi was also surprisingly immediate. He was deemed "worthy" of his only daughter in very short order. In turn, Robi admired Father and, most importantly, was not intimidated by him. They quickly developed a friendship and forged a bond of affection and trust.

"Take care of my little Zsuzsi," I heard my Father say to Robi not long before we announced that we wanted to get married. I still remember Robi's pledge, "I will."

At the time I thought this droll, even charming. In retrospect, I should not have. It came back to haunt me about ten or twelve years into our seemingly idyllic marriage. The proverbial handwriting was on the wall, but neither of us saw it until it was too late.

11. Marriage

In 1952, life was good and I was content, as long as I did not think about the future, and most of the time I didn't. At nineteen, even at twenty, there was no pressing reason to do so, and plenty of reasons for not doing so under the circumstances. Romance was great, but marriage was the last thing on my mind. I hardly noticed that we were gliding inevitably closer and closer to it.

After our frequent visits to Siofok, Robi thought that I should meet his mother as well. She and his grandmother issued an invitation for dinner. I wanted to make a good impression so I dressed carefully and made sure that everything I wore was neat and ironed. I hated ironing and avoided it whenever possible. I have no idea what I wore, except that it was neat and ironed.

Robi lived in a smallish, darkish apartment in the central part of the city on Kadar Street. In addition to the bedrooms, there was a living room and a formal dining room. The smell of cooking drifted from the kitchen. Robi's mother greeted us in the entrance hall. She was still a strikingly beautiful—if careworn—woman with dark wavy hair, a round face, and large soulful eyes. I thought she was somewhere in her early fifties. I was welcomed in a pleasant but formal manner. I think she may have been as nervous as I was. Soon after our introductions we sat down to dinner. Grandmother, a tiny dried up woman with a sour face, emerged from the kitchen and served the meal. She did all the cooking. Mami was a skilled seamstress who had worked from home ever since her husband had died.

I felt uncharacteristically self-conscious. This was so different from the informal family relationships I was accustomed to. I tried to be on my best behavior. I tried to eat all the not-so-great food put on my plate, and I tried to answer all their probing questions about my background and intentions as diplomatically as I could. I was careful not to make jokes or laugh too much. It was a somewhat somber occasion. The two women were not unfriendly, but they were not exactly warm and fuzzy either. That was not in their nature. They spoke mostly about what a wonderful son Robi was. It took me a little while to catch on, because they did not call him Robi. They addressed him and consistently referred to him as "Ocsi," or "Little Brother," a common nickname in Hungary for children with an older brother. Robi was almost twenty-four years old, six feet tall, and an assistant professor. He had not had an older brother for more than ten years now. I had a very hard time not making a comment, but I saw the warning in Robi's eyes in time and managed to keep my mouth shut and not inquire who Ocsi was.

In spite of my forebodings, Robi, aka Little Brother, reported that the evening was a success.

"Mami likes you," he told me. "Naturally, I knew she would," he added gallantly.

Grandmother was not mentioned. She was against Robi dating anyone, ever, on principle. She didn't like people very much, including her family, although she was fiercely loyal to them nevertheless.

I found out later that her attitude toward me was twofold. First, she and Mami could see that we genuinely loved and liked each other and their son was happy. Secondly, I was young, four years younger than Robi and appeared to be inexperienced, respectful, and in their view easily controlled.

None of these thoughts crossed my mind then—I was just happy that the visit was over. I would periodically tease my love, calling him Little Brother, which was rather mean I know, but hard to resist. Especially when he was holding forth in his professorial mode. At times, I would threaten to divulge his nickname to his friends and colleagues, but naturally, I never did.

Everything seemed good and I was content, as content as my restless nature would allow me to be. I was very much in love, but I did not exactly have an overwhelming desire to get married or settle down into blissful domesticity and then produce children. Oh, I did want children eventually, but not now, not yet. There was still so much else to do: get back to school, somehow, eventually, and become a writer, scholar, philosopher, or whatever I was meant to be. Produce great things, save the world. I did not lack fantasies of grandeur. Not that I believed them. But I had an ambition to learn, to develop whatever talents I had to the fullest. I wanted to find a direction and develop realistic goals. I needed to put my life back on track. Unrealistic as it was under the circumstances, I passionately wanted to escape the narrow confines of the present, to travel and see the world, to find freedom. I was a teeming mass of amorphous dreams, hopes, and wants.

So why on earth did we rock the boat—why did we decide to get married? It seems to me now, as it seemed to me then, that we kind of slid into it. We landed in matrimony as inevitably as the Danube ends in the Black Sea...

Perhaps it was a matter of convenience. Robi now spent most nights with me. It was hard for him to get up at the crack of dawn or in the small hours of the night and go home, get dressed, and go to work. He was sleep-deprived most of the time. It was hard for me to watch him go and not to be able to cuddle in the morning and have breakfast together. It was difficult to juggle the logistics of when and where we'd meet every day. I was relatively free apart from work, but Robi had to struggle to accommodate the needs and demands of his family.

It did not help that it was very difficult not to get pregnant. Contraceptives had not yet been invented and other forms of birth control were either unacceptable or rudimentary and largely ineffective. At age nineteen, I definitely did not want to get pregnant. Nor was Robi ready to become a father, but it felt less of a problem for him. It was not the first time that I felt faintly resentful about the "unfair" biological and social burdens of being female. Not only did we have to cope with often painful and debilitating monthly periods, but we also had to face the practically unavoidable lifelong consequences of sexuality such as becoming pregnant prematurely before we were ready. It was all quite scary and I came very close to giving up on sex altogether. Much later, I realized the unique blessings of being female and concluded that they mostly counterbalanced the disadvantages.

"I want to be with you more—I want to be with you all the time," Robi declared and I knew that I wanted the same thing. "We love each other and we want to spend our lives together. There is absolutely no reason for us not to get married, and every reason to do so," he said in his customary, logical way.

"Our parents think so too," he added for emphasis. I knew this was true.

"I am not even twenty yet, it is not clear what I want to do when I grow up…"

"You do want to be with me, don't you?" asked my beloved, and there was only one answer to that.

"We don't have anywhere to live, in any case!" I added for good measure, hoping to clinch the argument.

I should have known that Robi already had a plan. He always did.

"We can live at home with Mami and Grammy. They said they'd like that."

"You know we can't. The place is too small. There is no room for another person," was all I could say. What I could not and did not say was that I didn't want to move in with Mami and Grammy. I did not know exactly why, but it did not feel right. In fact, it felt downright scary. I was relieved when Robi agreed that the apartment was not big enough for the addition of a newly married couple. That should be the end of that, I thought. It only shows how little I knew my beloved.

"I think we should get engaged, anyway," Robi said sometime after this.

I did not see any harm in that. It was lovely and exciting. Our families and friends were happy. It was an acknowledgment of our belonging together. Nothing had changed, nothing had to be done. Everything was going to be just fine. I don't remember when I got the ring. I wish I did. It was a very beautiful ring of white gold with a large sapphire in the middle, surrounded by luminous small diamonds. It belonged to Mami, my future mother-in-law. I was deeply touched. To the best of my knowledge, I had never owned a ring until then. I don't remember ever having worn one. This was definitely a serious, grown-up ring. Like my mother's before it was exchanged for a goose and other edibles. I was now duty bound to wear this beautiful thing all the time. The ring seemed to possess a life of its own and it brought about profound changes that took me by surprise. It turned our internal commitment into an external one. Our personal relationship became an intrinsic part of two extended families and all of our friends. I felt happy and uneasy and vaguely domesticated, as if I had joined some kind of adult club. Overall, feelings of happiness prevailed. We did not have to sneak around anymore. We were now completely legit.

There were celebrations and Meetings of Families. Mine was small, just parents and the two remaining uncles and their wives. Robi's was a bit more numerous, in spite of the heavy loss of lives during the Holocaust. I remember in particular two of his aunts, Mami's sisters, and a much younger cousin. They were hard workers who were struggling to take care of their families under very difficult circumstances. Only one male had survived and he was traumatized and impaired, gradually becoming a recluse and a hoarder. He never threw out a newspaper or anything else. Their small apartment became impassable and a fire hazard. This wasn't considered weird or pathological then, as it would be today. The war never seemed to end for many of us "survivors." The need to save and preserve was often overwhelming, and the fear of starvation and freezing in the cold without adequate clothing was omnipresent even ten years after the war ended. But newspapers? I didn't know anyone else who felt passionate about preserving newspaper. I rather liked Robi's uncle.

Mami was the "lucky" sister chosen to take care of their mother, the matriarch. As it turned out, "manage" or "endure" would be a better way to put it. I found her a determined and controlling presence. Family lore had it that she had a talent for organizing and running things. They had owned a profitable restaurant before the war, its success due in large part to her heroic and relentless efforts. I wish I knew more about the family's history, but in typical teenage fashion I was too busy living my own life. Not until later did I develop a profound interest in other people's history, the only exception being fictional characters.

What happened next should have been predictable, but I did not see it coming. Not in the near future anyway.

One beautiful sunny day after work my betrothed showed up smiling like the Cheshire cat.

"I have great news," he announced as he executed an extra nice hug.

"Umm," I countered snuggling up closer. Then, as now, I was a sucker for good news, let alone great news!

"We have an apartment. We can get married!"

"You have an apartment. It is too small for all of us," I reminded him.

"No! We have an apartment. It is big enough for all of us present and future inhabitants." He actually winked when he said "future inhabitants."

"We have a beautiful, large apartment in the 11th district in Buda. Just across the bridge in Bercsenyi ucca," he added helpfully.

I was dumbfounded. This was impossible, a silly joke. There were no apartments available in Budapest and when they were, they were not affordable, unless, of course, you were a Communist Party dignitary. The housing shortage was still at its post-war peak, which is why multiple generations were jammed together, forced to live on top of each other, often in not-so-peaceful proximity.

Robi was not joking. This was for real. He and Mami and Grandmother had conspired to make an exchange. They had kept it quiet until it materialized. They had traded their very convenient inner-city apartment in Pest for a more spacious one, a little further out in Buda. Naturally, it cost money. I never found out how much or where the money came from, except that the bulk of it seemed to involve his parents.

"I want you to see it! Our room has lots of light. I know you love light. And it is in Buda! You love Buda. You grew up in Buda!"

He looked at me expectantly. I smiled, not wanting to disappoint him. I was feeling confused and overwhelmed. I did not feel the unmitigated enthusiasm he clearly expected. Why didn't I? It did not make any sense. Robi had presented me with a great gift. Sure, it was a fait accompli, a done deal, and I had not been consulted, but so what? Perhaps he wasn't either? Perhaps, he just wanted to surprise me? It was obvious that he was doing his best to make me happy. He loved me. I had to appreciate all the trouble he had gone to so we could marry. And so I did.

Only much, much later, as this pattern repeated itself over time, did I begin to slowly understand how much I disliked being presented with decisions made by Robi without any, or at best cursory, consultation. They were always in my "best interest" and therefore could not be challenged. The few times I did, I ended up feeling guilty for not appreciating him properly.

Today we would call this "The Tyranny of Love" but at age nineteen, that was beyond my grasp. I believe it was beyond his grasp, too.

Still, the magic persisted. Soon I forgot about the moments of doubt and indecision. Everybody was so very happy for us. We were a "beautiful couple." Everyone said so. I was a very fortunate person. Everyone said so. And it was true. I was in love and was very much loved in return. I had found my soul mate. I had found my lover. This was the Real Thing!

We started to plan our wedding. This wasn't especially difficult. The options were few. Church and synagogue weddings were forbidden and had to be held in private, more or less secretly. Neither of us was observant, but it was important to our families and it was an act of defiance against the regime. It turned out to be a depressing, furtive affair. There were lookouts to make sure we weren't being followed. Only the immediate family was present and a Rabbi, of course, whom we had never met before. For me, it was a reminder that we were still persecuted, endangered, held captive. Freedom still eluded us. Yet we were joined in matrimony according to ancient rites we have mostly forgotten. Our parents wept, then showered us with congratulations and love. We all left as soon as we could.

The official wedding was in the City Hall of Budapest. There was a very large room for that purpose that seated several hundred people. The walls were decorated with large frescoes in the monstrous style known as Socialist Realism. We were surrounded by gigantic, stilted figures of farmers wielding sickles or driving tractors in flowing embroidered white shirts; peasant girls in native costumes smiling inanely and carrying baskets overflowing with freshly harvested stalks of wheat, apples, grapes and singing merrily; and heroic, muscular, half-naked factory workers forging steel in the bowels of the earth. Think Diego Rivera, colorblind and suffering from dementia. It was a stilted, soulless place, but it was transformed into a happy one by our festive friends, loving families, and the joy and appreciation flowing to us from all sides.

I chose Dvořák's Humoresque as our Wedding March. I thought it appropriate under the circumstances. Robi wasn't so sure, but he agreed. The crowd roared with merriment as we walked down the aisle to those mocking tunes. Robi, tall and formal with blazing red hair and freckles, towered over me. I wore a little white suit and heels and a tiny thing of a hat with a pretend slip of a veil over my cropped dark hair. All unaccustomed finery, but it was fun. Sort of. Everybody loved us. It was the beginning of my domestication as it were. I have pictures to prove it.

A reception followed, but I can't quite remember where it was. It certainly wasn't at City Hall. There were lots of people there, most

Wedding ceremony in City Hall. Robi & I taking our wedding oaths, with Uncle Rezso as witness.

of whom I did not know. There were also presents of cherished heirlooms that neither of us wanted nor had room for. The only thing I remember with any clarity is a beautiful, ornately gilded hand-painted porcelain bowl that ignited my imagination and took me back to the Italian Renaissance.

I remember that I felt intensely uncomfortable. I was not used to this much attention. I had problems with crowds. I felt nauseous and had a nasty headache. I had lots of headaches when I was young. Robi noticed that something was wrong. Forever protective, he spirited me upstairs to rest until we could sneak away and get on the train for our honeymoon.

All honeymoons are special, but I considered ours exceptionally exotic, extraordinarily fantastic. Ok, so it wasn't the Riviera or Easter Island, or even Mexico. It was Sopron, aka Oldenburg, on the border with Austria. Let me repeat this: on the border with Austria! It was the next best thing to going abroad. Neither of us had ever been abroad.

Robi had gone to a great deal of trouble to get us there. Ordinary citizens were not allowed to visit the border region, lest they find a way to escape the vast prison that was Hungary. In spite of the minefields, barbed wire fences, and watchtowers filled with armed border guards, the "Government of the People for the People," as they liked to call themselves, clearly didn't trust its people. In any case, Robi managed to "pull some strings" using his faculty rank and God knows what else, and got us a week's sojourn in this paradise.

Sopron is a charming small town dating back to Roman times. It is tucked into the foothills of the Alps, surrounded by prized vineyards, untamed forests, and mountains. At the time, in spite of the ubiquitous Roman ruins, it had a vaguely mysterious, medieval air,

*Communing with the bishop
on our honeymoon in Sopron.*

with twisting narrow cobblestone lanes and ancient crumbling houses. Statues dotted the public squares and there were abandoned archeological excavations from the Roman to the medieval and baroque periods. I was particularly fond of a statue of an unnamed bishop who seemed to have a cheerful disposition. It seemed to me that he approved of Robi and me hugging him affectionately. Miraculously, I still have a picture of this, in case you don't believe me.

Our accommodations were not luxurious, but then we were not used to luxurious. We were assigned a dormitory room on campus since it was summer and no students were in attendance. It was a long, narrow, light-filled room that had a steel twin bed with a lumpy old mattress and a window. No room service. Who cared. We had a ball. When we got tired of indoors, we roamed the town, climbed the mountains, built campfires, and drank the local wine. And ate, of course. We searched out local food and occasionally sampled some of the more affordable restaurants.

It was a wonderful honeymoon. For the first time we were able to spend our days and nights together, just the two of us, without interference. It was pure, unadulterated happiness.

It would not happen again for a very long time and then, only intermittently. Places, like people, sometimes assume special significance in your life. They not only shape your experience but become active participants in it. They become agents of transformation. Sopron was such a place for me. A gate to my married life as well as a gate to freedom. We returned to Sopron to cross the mountains not quite three years later, in the fall of 1956. This magical place allowed us to escape "slavery" and reach the "Promised Land," or at least Austria.

12. After the Honeymoon and the Birth of Andrea

Alas, honeymoons don't last forever and neither does "happily ever after," but we did not know that at the time. In any case, we had to leave behind beautiful, magical Sopron and start our married life in our new communal home.

Moving to Bercsenyi Street was easy, as I had very few belongings. I found, though, that it was hard to think of it as my home. It was really Robi's home, mine only insofar as Robi and I constituted a unit. We had one large sunny room of our own, with a double door, in the back of the apartment. It was this room that I considered my home. The rest contained all the furniture, rugs, pictures, crystals, vases, and other belongings of Mami's that had somehow survived the war. It was all unfamiliar, representing the memories of lives unknown to me. Robi almost never talked about the past, about his childhood. Mami and Grammy had small bedrooms and all four of us had to share a bathroom, which resulted in frequent traffic jams, especially in the mornings. Luckily there was an extra lavatory down the hall. Grammy and Mami were in charge of the household. They ruled over everything, especially the kitchen.

I was banned in general, except for helping to clean up after a meal, and then I was expected to follow precise instructions. Granted, I did not know much about cooking, but it would have been nice to experiment, to have been part of the team. I could cook eggs in all their splendid variations, and I could heat up leftovers, or make toast. Sandwiches were easy. Open-faced with butter and salami, or bologna, or hard sausage with mustard. Sometimes there would be cheese, smelly or otherwise, with a touch of paprika. Robi and I loved the smelly cheese, and boy, was it smelly!

In the evenings, we all ate together whenever possible, which was most of the time. The menu was simple, depending very much on what was available and affordable in the shops and the market. That meant lots of soup, casseroles, potato dishes, and pasta, and sometimes rice. On weekends we had chicken. Mami and Grammy were very frugal. I wasn't. Even though I had very little money, I loved to spend what I had on gifts. I often picked up extra goodies when I could find them, such as choice cold cuts, smoked sausage and bacon, good Pick Salami, fresh ham, a bar of chocolate, or some good fresh bread or rolls, which were great favorites and often hard to come by.

Mami appreciated it, but Grammy thought I was profligate, wasteful, and spoiled. She did not actually say any of those things, but I could sense her disapproval. I suspected that she did not care much for chocolate, or for me. I don't remember her baking much either, come to think of it.

In fact, I remember precious little about my first year in the Darvas household. Conversation was sparse and usually centered around the logistics of everyday living. There were no harsh words or raised voices, ever. Robi and I avoided open conflict by the simple method of doing as we were told and not insisting on controlling any aspect of the routine of the household. Robi was quite used to this and I simply fell in line with him. None of this was very difficult, but in many ways, I felt like a guest who was expected to contribute a little, give a hand cleaning up after meals, help with dishes, do my own laundry and ironing, but otherwise stay out of the way.

The biggest problem was the lack of privacy. During the week, Robi and I worked long hours, but we were expected to be home for dinner and be sociable. Even after we retired to our room, the closed door was not always respected, or approved of. Robi tried to do something about this, but he was not entirely successful. Even on weekends, when we tried to sleep in, cuddle and do the things couples do, we were frequently interrupted by loud calls, or insistent knocking on the door if we didn't respond immediately. At least there were knocks now, a great improvement over previous unannounced intrusions. Robi was in great demand. From changing a light bulb to fixing a faucet, his assistance and advice were continually sought in every area of the family's existence.

We did not want to be unsociable or hurt anybody's feelings, so over time the two of us were forced to start dating again. We needed time to talk, to spend some time exclusively with each other. We met in cafes or wandered along the Danube or the brightly lit boulevards. In wintertime we shared a bag of chestnuts roasted over an open charcoal fire from street vendors. Sometimes, but not often, we went out for dinner alone, or with friends. We always made sure to bring home goodies, for we understood that Mami and Grammy felt hurt by our absence, meaning of course Robi's absence.

I felt quietly resented, tolerated, but certainly not loved. I might be wrong, but I don't think so.

Things changed once I got pregnant a little more than a year into our marriage. It was not exactly a planned pregnancy for we were ambivalent about bringing a child into a world we were both struggling to cope with, a world of oppression, danger, and privation. Also a world where three or more generations would be obliged to live together in peace and harmony.

In spite of these misgivings, the appearance of our first child on the world stage was met with unmitigated approval. No, that does not do it justice. It was greeted with tremendous joy and excitement by all. It was like the whole world was applauding and smiling with excitement and delight. My parents were ecstatic, and Mami and Grammy's generally grim countenances softened into frequent smiles, as I was increasingly recognized as the future mother of their grandchild. Robi, who was always loving and caring, became overwhelmingly protective and thoughtful.

I was stunned when I first realized I was pregnant. I had had irregular periods before and I had seen an Ob-Gyn for various complaints. He was a highly respected but old-fashioned doctor. He was convinced that all my complaints would vanish once I got pregnant. He believed that the body of a healthy, sexually active young woman rebelled against not being allowed to bear children by developing pathology in the reproductive tracts. It was the 1950s version of holistic medicine. Naturally, I thought it was voodoo medicine, or that he must have been joking. Perhaps he was. In any case, when he informed Robi and me of our imminent parenthood, I was totally unprepared.

I had always wanted to have children and I wanted children with Robi. Sometime in the future. When we were older. Underneath all the bravado, I felt like I was hardly more than a child myself. I was twenty-one and I was about to become a mother. It felt like entering a different reality, and in many ways, this was true. I was awestruck, scared, delighted, and amazed all at the same time. This was the grand adventure of my life. I was going to become the best possible mother to this best possible child, still just a speck of cells beginning to grow in my womb. I felt a great surge of love and new hope as Robi and I embraced, and the transformation from the still new roles of husband and wife to those of father and mother began.

The first six weeks of pregnancy were difficult as my body rebelled against accepting the presence of the stranger. My hormones were surging and my digestive system turned topsy-turvy. I was nauseated and food turned me off. When I did eat, the food did not stay with me very long. I was not allowed to lift or carry anything. Pregnant women were protected against even the mildest forms of physical exertion or exercise for fear of miscarriage. Except for peasants or laborers of course. Even in that supposedly classless society some people were more coddled then others.

Robi started to hover around me anxiously. If I happened to mention at 11 o'clock at night that anchovies or chocolate-covered cherries seemed appealing, he would dash out to the only 24-hour supermarket in town to get them. When the doctor ordered a glass of Tokaji Aszu every day to bolster my red blood cells, he moved heaven and earth to obtain it. It was not an easy task. Tokaji Aszu was, and still is, a rare and very expensive Hungarian dessert wine aged to perfection over years, even decades. And yes, the doctors thought it was a good idea for a somewhat anemic pregnant woman to have a glass every day.

I was ordered to rest as much as possible. Robi did not let me move around and enforced this by hovering around anxiously whenever he was nearby. It was actually a relief to go to work, but even there I was surrounded with exaggerated support and care. Commuting got a lot easier. I didn't have to stand and be jostled about in the bus or the tram anymore. At the sight of my bulging belly, men and teenagers would jump up and offer their seats. The funny thing was that by the time my pregnancy was clearly visible, I felt a lot better and did not really need any special treatment. Not that I didn't enjoy the attention.

Unformed and unseen, our baby instantaneously became a major presence in our lives, as the sudden sprouting of a new life transformed our universe. We tried to imagine what our baby would look like. Was it going to be a she or a he? There was no way of knowing, since there were no tests or sonograms in those days. We decided we didn't care as long as the baby was healthy. I secretly hoped for a little girl as a first child, because I thought I remembered my own childhood sufficiently to help bring up a girl, whereas I had never been around little boys. I was willing to learn, though. I had to learn a lot anyway.

We started thinking about names. Everybody in the family had preferences and thoughtful suggestions. We decided to ignore them all. It was easier that way, showing that we did not pick favorites. We ourselves had a few criteria. The child had to have a "universal" name. It had to be easily transferable to any language, or at least to most western languages, without major changes. This was important. We hoped that the next generation would have access to the wider world.

Names of living relatives were out of the question, since Jewish custom did not allow it. There was pressure from Mami to name the baby Tibor, if a boy, after Robi's brother. I felt uncomfortable naming a baby after someone who had already departed from this existence, someone who was marked by death at a young age who never made it out of the concentration camp and who was murdered as a teenager. Although we had never met, I loved and wanted to remember Tibor, because Robi had loved him very deeply. Yet I did not want my child, our child, to carry the burden of Tibor's life as well as his own. In any case, the issue was moot, as we ended up with a daughter.

Andrea was born on March 27, 1956, at the venerable Rokus (St. Roche) Hospital in Budapest, after a largely uneventful pregnancy. Rokus was considered the best, most advanced medical facility in Budapest at the time. It had been around for over 200 years and had a distinguished history. But it definitely showed its age. The yellow and white exterior paint was peeling and the façade was pockmarked from bombs and artillery fire. Inside, long, winding corridors led to large communal wards separated by gender. The maternity ward was not soundproof and moans and screams of birthing mothers were audible, if somewhat muted. It was not a reassuring place.

Andrea took her time emerging from her cozy if cramped nesting place, my womb. She was two weeks late and the doctor decided to induce labor. It was a long labor—over two days. In the end, the surgeon decided to intervene and use "high forceps" to pull the baby from the birth canal, as she appeared to be stuck and getting entangled in the umbilical cord. It was a risky procedure, but not quite as risky as a Caesarean section would have been. In those days a Caesarean was used only as a last resort. Vacuum extraction did not yet exist.

All in all, it was a scary and painful process for which I was mostly unprepared. My mother and Mami had not been willing or able to provide me with information ahead of time. Pregnancy and childbirth were not discussed in polite company. There were no books or childbirth classes and the Lamaze method wasn't used until the late 1950s. The family was not allowed to participate in birthing and I was alone during the whole process, except for the nurses, who offered periodic care and instructions, and the doctor, who popped in once or twice a day to assure me that all was well, even when it wasn't. Communication between medical staff and patients was rather limited in those days.

I knew that all this must be very difficult for Robi as well. It was his nature to problem solve and help. But all he could do was wait.

He had absolutely no control over events. We had no way to communicate. Cell phones were nonexistent, even in one's most fevered imagination!

I felt isolated and very much alone in this fight to deliver a new life. Nobody had told me how bad it could get. All my energy was concentrated on both of us surviving. If it occurred to me that things could go wrong, I refused to consider it, even when the odds started looking bad. My doctor was paged and he decided on immediate surgical intervention. The last thing I remember before blacking out was a chorus of "Push, Push, Push" and I pushed with all my might until everything went dark.

Waking from anesthesia I was informed that I had a beautiful, active, healthy little girl. Through the haze of exhaustion I remember an unearthly sense of relief and joy. I looked around for Robi as I was wheeled out of the operating room, but he was not allowed in the recovery area. Instead it was the portly, fatherly surgeon whose beaming face and booming voice congratulated me on a successful delivery. The nurses pointed out that he deserved most of the credit. Evidently his timely and highly skilled surgical intervention had saved the baby and most likely me. I thanked him. He accepted it graciously. He said I had a lot to do with it too. I gave a barely perceptible nod.

"What is it that you want most at this moment?" he asked, feeling generous and prepared for some profound response.

I had no doubt in my mind. "I want a cigarette and I want to see my husband and my baby." The first request was highly irregular request, even in those days, but at that moment of amazed relief I wanted one more than anything else.

I got my cigarette, but I had to wait quite a long time to see my husband and my baby. There were "procedures" to be followed after all.

Once I had been settled in my bed on the ward, my vital signs checked, and my head propped up, baby made her appearance. She was tightly swaddled in hospital-grade flannel blankets, her little face flushed and all puckered up, her miniature hands clenched into tiny fists, her fingers hardly bigger then matchsticks. She looked so very fragile I hardly dared to touch her, but I did hold her, very, very cautiously. She needed to feed, but she didn't know how. I wasn't much help either. We were both new at this game. Finally, with a nurse's help, we guided her to the nipple and she grabbed it with unexpected determination.

"Ouch! That hurts!" I recoiled. It was an automatic response. The baby lost the nipple. She started crying. I could not blame her. We tried again and again and finally we both caught on and she got some colostrum. I didn't know what it was, but it looked weird. Yellow, not like milk at all. I was upset and exhausted. The nurses decided they could do a better job feeding the baby and took her away. I fell into a deep sleep. I did not dream.

When I woke up, Robi was there and it felt good. It was the first time we had been together since I went into labor. The world had changed. We were now mother and father. We had a daughter. I know it happens all the time, but for us it was momentous. Life changing, to put it mildly. We hugged and we kissed and we cried. We decided to call her Andrea rather than Judit, the name we had originally planned for a girl. Our reason? I just thought that she looked more like an Andrea and Robi agreed. I think he would have agreed to anything at that point. I don't think he ever got over not being the one to have given birth. I sometimes wonder if most men didn't carry a permanent grudge about not being capable of growing a new life and giving birth. Perhaps that's why they overcompensate, why they have to persistently prove their superiority? I don't know.

Many years later, when the subject came up, Robi dismissed the idea. "No, it's not like that at all. Women are more like a vending machine. You drop in your quarter and the Coke pops out, or candy, or whatever…" He said it with a mischievous grin, but I sensed that he was not entirely joking.

I was in the hospital for almost two weeks because of the birth complications. This was much longer than the standard five days. I saw Andrea four or five times a day at designated feeding times only. I got to hold her and snuggle with her, but only briefly. The focus was on providing nourishment, and that did not go smoothly. Even after the initial few days I did not have much milk and the baby went hungry.

This was very upsetting. I felt like a failure. The women around me in the ward were happily breastfeeding their babies. But my body simply refused to produce enough milk, and soon it stopped entirely. My breasts got so sore that I got an infection. What to do? Andrea did not respond well to formula, which was then at a fairly primitive stage of development and in short supply. We, that is Robi and my mother, found a nursing mother with an abundant supply of milk who was willing to provide us with her excess production of the precious substance for a price. It was picked up fresh every day and Andrea began to thrive. We could go home.

Mami had everything ready for us at home. Baby clothes, cradle, diapers, everything. She not only showed me how and when to change the baby, she insisted on doing so herself. I did not object in the beginning. I was still weak and the baby poop made me nauseous. I had never seen a baby before, let alone changed one. Babies wore cloth diapers that had to be rinsed and thrown into the laundry basket to be washed and boiled and dried for future use. Yep, I did throw up. I am not proud of it, but I did.

I felt profoundly inadequate. As a mother, I should have known how to do all these things well. I kept trying and gradually made good progress, but it was not easy to persuade my in-laws to hand over caretaking duties. They were much more experienced and better at it, after all! They were being helpful, so how could I fight them? I wasn't breastfeeding, so I was not even needed for feeding the baby. I nevertheless did, whenever I had the chance. It was an ongoing struggle.

Sterilizing the bottles and nipples involved boiling them on the stove and was definitely my task. Robi and I decided to take charge of bathing Andrea in the evening. Grudgingly Mami and Grandma agreed, but they reserved the right to supervise.

Robi went about planning it with scientific precision. He laid out the towels on a folding table by the bathroom sink, which was filled with lukewarm water. Later we had a small tub on top of the table where our wiggling little daughter would be submerged with only her head held up above water, chirping happily. I was always afraid that the slippery, wiggly little body would slip from my hands, but it never did. Besides, Robi was there to help out if necessary. Not that he knew anything more about babies than I did, but at least he acted as though he did, and his mother accepted his authority. Bathing baby Andrea became our nightly routine. It was our special time together for the three of us.

Soon I was back to work, happy but seriously sleep deprived. I was usually on night duty since Robi was the primary breadwinner and we all agreed that he had to be both on time and alert for his more demanding work. Not that he didn't help out. Often, if I was too exhausted, he would pick up Andrea and bring her to me to feed. Sometimes he would even heat up the bottle, a somewhat involved business. We had to warm up the water in a pan and put in the bottle until it became warm enough. If it was not warm enough, the baby would get colicky, and if it was too warm, she would refuse to touch it. Robi developed a system that worked most of the time.

Andrea emerged into our bizarre little world at the end of March and had a lot to cope with from the beginning. Her first three months were especially rough. She had to recover from the trauma of an unusually tough birth and she had an underdeveloped digestive system. She was colicky and uncomfortable much of the time and she slept very little and furtively. She still managed to be alert, active, happy, and loving, probably because she was surrounded by adoring, responsive parents and grandparents and had a reasonably well-structured routine.

Naturally, it was not going to last. We were in Hungary, after all.

On October 23, 1956, university students and other young intellectuals staged a peaceful demonstration, demanding freedom of speech, freedom of the press, the end of political persecution, and the removal of Soviet troops from Hungarian soil. Initial negotiations failed after the Hungarian leaders calling for independence were lured to a meeting and arrested. Their leader, Imre Nagy, and many of his cohort were executed. The Freedom Fighters decided to fight. Soviet troops started moving in and the revolution turned violent. Budapest was under siege once again.

In my short life so far this seemed to have become a recurring event.

This time Soviet troops were not fighting Hitler, but ordinary Hungarian citizens: workers, teachers, writers, students, and everyone else who had enough of Stalinist terror, which was pretty much the whole country and very much included me. We wanted the freedom to say and think and read what we wanted, to bring up our children as we saw fit, to take back our country. The need for autonomy, on both the personal and societal levels, is a very powerful thing. People were and still are willing to risk their lives for it. It is a never-ending story.

The anti-Stalinist uprisings had started in Poland earlier in the year, spread to Czechoslovakia, and finally reached Hungary in October. It had started peacefully enough with demonstrations; people were demanding freedom of speech and an elected democratic government. They wanted Russian troops out of their countries. What were they still doing there, ten years after they had liberated us from the Germans, ten years after WWII had ended?

We had exchanged German occupation for Soviet occupation, clumsily hidden behind an indigenous puppet government. Was the country better off? Perhaps, marginally. Jews were not singled out for extinction, as they had been under the Nazis. Persecution under the Soviets was more democratic and inclusive. You did not have to be a Jew for the Secret Police (AVO) to show up in the middle of the night and drag you—or your father or brother, or sometimes the whole family—away, never to be seen again. You didn't have to be a Jew to lose your job or your property, or to be deported. You didn't have to be a Jew to be muzzled, disciplined, denied a decent job or living wages, or forbidden to express opinions if they diverged from the party line.

On the other hand, until then there had been no active fighting on the streets and you did not have to hide in air raid shelters. You could live, if you were lucky, in a cramped, bomb-damaged apartment with other families you had never met before. There was public transportation of sorts, and running water, at least in the cities, and electricity.

Hungary was about to reenact its famous 1848 Revolution,

dubbed the Freedom Fight (Szabadsagharc), which had happened just about a century before. That revolution, which was against the Hapsburg Empire, had ended in dismal defeat, destruction, and a renewed wave of terror. The best of the best were killed, exiled, obliterated. History tends to repeat itself with tiresome regularity.

This was a losing battle and everyone knew it. The more credulous hoped for Western intervention. They hoped to become a new, "neutral Austria." As though the West was likely to risk another World War for this tiny, troublesome country! As though they were not too busy fighting for their interests in the Suez Canal.

There was a lot of mortar fire in the last few days of the 1956 revolution and Russian tanks took their positions on the streets. Once again we spent most of our time in the cellar. Once again it doubled as a shelter, dark, damp, spooky. Except now I had a baby. Food supplies were depleted rapidly, including formula for Andrea. This was a big problem. What to do? Robi, the fittest, hardiest and only male member of this extended family of women, could not go outside. All young males were shot on sight by Russian soldiers on the grounds that they could be Freedom Fighters!

There was really only one solution. You guessed it. Yours truly, age 22, not much of a fighter or hiker, took a deep breath and stepped out into the fray—the streets. It is amazing how your body takes over security operations in times of danger. Instantly I was dodging bullets, running from doorway to doorway and judging instinctively how to avoid danger at every step until I reached my destination— the pharmacy, which was still open for a few hours a few days of the week. There was no time to register fear for more than seconds. I had to make instantaneous decisions to avoid getting killed.

My whole being concentrated on reaching the goal, in this case getting formula and baby food, and surviving long enough to get them home. I may not have been able to provide her with mother's milk, but I was lucky and always managed to get the food she needed to survive.

By November 4, 1956, Russian tanks had extinguished all opposition and the revolution was over! We were facing a reign of terror once again.

Andrea was seven months old.

13. Escape

Today is November 20, 2016. This date probably does not mean much to you, but it is very important nevertheless. It was exactly sixty years ago that we, your grandparents, set out on the great adventure that defined not only the rest of our lives, but yours as well. After all, you would never have been born had it not been for what happened. I was twenty-two then. It has taken me a long time to tell you about it.

I find my age amazing, even incomprehensible. I don't own anything that is nearly as old as I am. Well, perhaps some photographs and a few mementos from my father. I also have my mother's small Hungarian prayer book with the pale sea-green mother of pearl cover hidden in some obscure drawer. What I mean is, I don't own anything nearly as old that still works. In contrast, the durability of the human body and soul amazes me. For example, my size 7.5 feet have carried me around with perfect ease for eighty-two long years. Actually, only 81, I guess, since it takes a while for a baby to learn to walk.

Anyway, we are back in Budapest in November 1956, sixty years ago, when my daughter was born, just seven months before the uprising against the Stalinist regime. Your grandfather Robi nicknamed her "Prucsok Hercegno" or Grasshopper Princess (OK, so it does not sound as good in English) because of her grace, beauty, constant chatter, sweet voice, and perpetual motion. She was born in a year of exceptional turmoil, even by Hungarian standards.

After the revolution ended, Hungarians were facing a reign of terror once again. On the bright side, electricity was more or less restored, if intermittent and rationed. There was running water again and credible rumors that some of the peasant farmers had made their way in their horse-drawn buggies to the big Central Market (Focsarnok) in Pest, on the other side of the river. This was great news if you didn't have any food left in the pantry, fresh or otherwise.

One blustery sunny day I set out for the Central Market, which was a longish hike across the bridge. I had a large backpack, hoping for a good haul. Sure enough, the market was teeming with vendors. People were fighting over the goods. With patience and perseverance, I managed to get the essentials in my backpack—flour, sugar, bread, vegetables, beans, and even some freshly pickled cucumbers—when I spotted one of the big prize items: a lovely large fifteen-pound goose! We had not seen the likes of it for several months. It would feed us for weeks and provide rendered fat for cooking and beautiful tasty cracklings to snack on. We would have wonderful baked goose liver for at least a week. Mami would make soup, a roast, and biscuits from renderings. Everyone would be so very happy.

Unfortunately, I was not the only one coveting it. I began to approach the stand cautiously. There were at least two dozen people competing for a couple of geese. There were no orderly lines. Hungarians did not believe in them. It was "may the best, meaning most aggressive, man or woman win." I was not strong enough to push through the crowd, but perhaps small enough to slip through it. I decided to give it a try. It worked. Suddenly I found myself right in front of a kindly heavy-set red-faced woman with a kerchief around her head. She decided to put the two remaining geese up for the highest bidder. It was a smart move on her part. She would get the most money and avoid a riot by the competing crowd. I put in a bid for one goose. I was bidding high and got the prize. It was like winning the lottery! I set out on the long journey home feeling triumphant and happy.

As it turned out, neither Robi nor I would see or taste the Feast of the Goose. I climbed the stairs to the apartment and entered, shouting triumphantly, "Look what I got!" There was no response, no triumphant welcome, only silence. An ominous hush had descended over the place. My husband and Jozsi K, his best friend, were huddled in the living room. I wondered how he had gotten there since it was still dangerous for young males to wander around the city. Mami hovered in the background, her face in a worried frown. I dropped the backpack bulging with food on the floor.

"What happened? Is the baby all right?" I asked.

The baby was fine.

"The word is out that a train might be leaving at dawn tomorrow from Keleti Station for the border in Sopron," said Jozsi. "It would be the first train leaving Budapest and it might be the last for quite a while. I have a letter here from Eva, a friend, asking me to come and get her. She has been stuck at the sanitarium for weeks now."

I stared at him.

"Jozsi thinks this is our chance to escape, to cross the border," Robi explained. "We have to make a decision now."

This was extremely risky business. Even under normal circumstances you needed special permits to enter the border region. Sopron was closer to the Austrian border than any other Hungarian town. These were not normal circumstances. We were under martial law. Even if there was actually a train leaving, even if we managed to get on that train, even if we were not removed, arrested, or deported to

Siberia because we had no permit, even if we got as far as Sopron, I saw no way to cross the border. A broad swath of terrain in the region had been converted to mine fields to prevent people from leaving. There were guard towers placed at regular intervals along the full length of the Austrian border—even through the mountains—with armed guards ready to kill. The whole country was a vast prison. The grapevine had it that while many of the Hungarian border guards had abandoned their stations, invading Soviet troops were in the process of replacing them.

I looked at Robi. "You know how much I hate it here, how I need to get out to save my sanity. I don't want my child to grow up in this crazy country, but you two must be out of your minds. There is no way we can pull this off."

Robi nodded, but Jozsi waved a piece of paper at me. It was the letter from Eva. "We can show this to the security guards. We can show them that we have an urgent reason to travel. She has a heart condition. She is worried about her parents. She does not dare to return to Budapest by herself."

I knew this was the flimsiest of excuses and did not think for a moment that the soldiers or security guards would buy it. Still, it was perhaps our only chance to get away, to escape from this nightmare of a country to freedom.

"Even if we make it to Sopron, how do you propose to get over the border? How on earth do you think we can get to Austria?" I asked Robi.

Jozsi had thought about this. Eva would find a local familiar with the terrain who could guide us through the mountains and avoid the active minefields and guard towers. For a price. It was a plan of sorts. Perhaps with a little luck it could work, I thought. You learned to trust in luck as a major survival tool during the war.

"How are we going to explain the baby?" I asked.

I was met with a blank stare.

"What baby?" Robi eventually said. He stood up and embraced me. "We can't possibly risk her life," he continued. "We may risk our own, but have no right risking hers. Besides, her cries would alert the border guards that we were attempting to escape during the night," he added, ever the pragmatic engineer. "It is simply not possible. Your mother and father can come and get her as soon as transportation becomes available. We either leave her with the grandparents, or we all stay. It is your decision."

And that was that. It became my decision. I understood that Robi could play it both ways. He was already an assistant professor of engineering at the university, a very good job. He had managed to stay politically "clean" so far. He could stay and survive, even prosper. He also knew that his skills as an engineer would be well appreciated in the West and that a far more interesting and challenging career would be possible for him, in addition to freedom. Robi was realistic and reasonable and had a talent for self-preservation. It was I who hated the regime with a passion and felt emotionally and professionally destroyed by it. Disenfranchised. Shut out from university, from my love of the theater, from free speech, from being human. It was I who did not think I could bring up my child amidst lies, discrimination and hatred. I ached for a better life for all of us. I believed that there was one, away from Hungary. I wanted, needed to take care of all of us. But taking care of my child by leaving her behind? Building her a better life by abandoning her? My mind was shutting down. The head of the prized goose peered at us dolefully from the backpack. I closed my eyes. The men were still looking at me when I reopened them.

In the end, I said yes and we decided to leave. The rest of that afternoon is a blur. We made telephone calls to my parents, coded in veiled language, to make sure they would take care of Andrea until we "returned from our trip." They understood. We also called Ellen and Jonah, our closest friends, to see if they wanted to join us. Ellen decided to stay because she was fearful and did not want to leave her parents behind. And here I was about to leave my baby behind! I believed with all my heart that I was doing this for her as much as for myself, that it was her only chance for a decent life. I never even considered failure, or not being able to rescue her within a very short period of time. Perhaps just as well. Knowing too much can often protect you or save you, but it can also prevent you from taking risks, from taking necessary action.

We were reasonably clear about the dangers. We weighed them against the chance for a free, autonomous life, a life worth living. For us and for our children. It was a prison break, except we were not the criminals. The criminals were the ones running the prisons. Come to think of it, all my life, danger and death had never been far away. They had been all around me ever since I could remember, usually superimposed by outside powers. Now, however, we made our own choice to face danger and risk.

The next morning, very early, we set out on foot for the train station. I hugged baby Andrea, but was careful not to wake her. She was sleeping blissfully after a very restless night. There was a mob at the station, but somehow, we managed to hook up with Jozsi. He was nervous but determined. There was no time for second thoughts as we were engulfed by the mob, fighting to secure a place on the train. There were many more people than room on the train, though it was a very long train. Nobody knew whether it would actually leave the station since no trains had been allowed to do so for several weeks. People were trying desperately to get home to their husbands, wives, and children, and to their everyday lives disrupted by events in the capital. There were many peasant farmers carrying their belongings in huge bundles on their backs. They were caught up in the revolution and cut off from their home base. They were eager to return and tend their farms and livestock. It was late autumn, so there was much to be done. But there were others like us, young city dwellers. We knew we could not carry anything across the border, even if we made it that far.

For show, to make ourselves credible, we each carried a small suitcase lightly filled with necessities—a sweater, a windbreaker, soap, a toothbrush and toothpaste, and small gifts for Eva, who was the supposed reason for our presence in Sopron. We kept on rehearsing our cover story over and over again. She had been in a sanitarium for over a month because of a mild heart condition. This was true. She wanted to come home to Budapest, but was reluctant to venture it alone given the political turmoil. A fact, if not particularly credible.

Anyway, we managed to get onto the train and for once did not mind being squeezed and jostled by the motley crowd. It afforded us a measure of anonymity. Most people were jittery but friendly. We all shared the same predicament, waiting nervously for the train to pull out of the station. After about two-and-a-half hours, it finally did. There were rumors that soldiers were entering the other cars asking for identifications. It turned out that they were Hungarian soldiers, not Soviets, which meant that the checks were perfunctory, pro forma. They were on our side and also heading for the border.

After five or six hours and a few tense stops, we arrived in Sopron. Hungry, thirsty, and urgently needing a toilet, but we arrived. It was very cold. Robi and I had rather special memories of our honeymoon in Sopron about two years before. Understandably, we resisted the temptation to revisit them. We headed for the hills to find the sanitarium. It turned out to be quite a hike from the train station. Some of the details are blurry now, but I remember it as a rather grand resort reserved for Party members and their families. Eva's family had good connections. We felt out of place and grubby in our hiking gear. We had made it this far but had no idea what would happen next or even where we would spend the night.

I had never actually met Eva before. Jozsi had kept her under wraps. We knew she was pursuing him, but he was reluctant, to say the least. I soon understood why. Jozsi's family was old gentry with democratic leanings. They had never supported the fascists and were persecuted and robbed by both them and the Communists. He was older than we, and he had managed to get a law degree during the post-war interlude when there was a moderate coalition government, before the Communists took over. He could not get a job after graduation, however, since the political situation had worsened. He was disenfranchised and living on the margin, in constant danger of being deported. Despite this, he was a soft-spoken, intelligent, gentle soul who bore his misfortunes with stoic dignity and impeccable manners. Eva was about his age, in her late twenties. She was tough, loud, and solidly built with a round face and coiffed blondish hair. She tended to be bossy, to put it kindly. Jozsi was a quiet philosopher, and Eva was a practical, domineering, sturdy doer. He seemed both fascinated and repelled by her brash and loud behavior, her sense of entitlement and unfortunate habit of putting people down.

Eva was happy to see us. We were greeted as her very own rescue squad. We had a light meal of roast chicken, potatoes, and fresh vegetables waiting for us. It was accompanied by an excellent, fragrant local wine. We enjoyed the feast, the likes of which we had not seen in Budapest for a very long time. We were hungry after our long trip and devoured everything gratefully. She also had bread, ham, and smoked sausages packed for our "hike," along with water and a canteen of schnapps for emergencies. We had flashlights, but no weapons and no maps.

It was impossible to get maps of the border region. Instead, Eva had arranged for a local guide who was willing to get us across the border for money. We all pitched in, of course. I don't know the exact sum; it was a hush-hush, clandestine transaction with much complex negotiation. In the end, we gave him all the money we had, plus the gold necklace with the ruby pendant I was wearing. I felt bad about the necklace, since it was the only thing I had left from my childhood. I did not care much about the money. After all, you could not use Hungarian forints in Austria or in Siberia, and definitely not if you were dead.

The guide's name was Jani, I think. It was probably not his real name. For all we knew, he might take us straight to the Communist authorities or to the Russians once we had paid, but we had to take the chance. He was a taciturn, unfriendly middle-aged guy with a pockmarked face and hooded eyes. He made me uneasy. He said that he knew the mountains like the back of his hand. He had lived and hunted around there all his life. He knew all the trails and mountain passes and would steer us away from the guard towers along the border. He was going to lead us safely through the mountains to Austria. It would be a long, tough hike, but some of the guard towers were occupied by Hungarian soldiers who would probably turn a blind eye, and many of the minefields were already cleared. We had to hurry, though, because Russian soldiers were moving in rapidly to replace the Hungarian border guards and they were reactivating minefields.

"How do we know who is who in the dark?" asked Robi.

"The ones who start shooting are the Russians," was Jani's

not-so-helpful reply.

We shrugged our shoulders. "Dumb question deserves a dumb reply" is an old Hungarian saying…

We changed into our hiking gear and put the food, water, flashlights, Swiss army knives, compass, first aid gear, and other essentials in the backpacks, leaving the suitcases behind. We set out after nightfall and managed to slip out unnoticed.

> Midway in our life's journey, I went astray
> from the straight road and woke to find myself
> alone in a dark wood. How shall I say
> what wood that was! I never saw so drear,
> so rank, so arduous a wilderness!
> Its very memory gives a shape to fear.
> (DANTE. *The Divine Comedy,* Inferno Canto 1,
> translated by John Ciardi)

I was certainly not near the middle of my life's journey, although at times like this it seemed I was getting pretty close to the end. Neither was I technically alone, with Robi and Jozsi and Eva. We were collectively alone in the dark and fearsome woods, with a not-so-dependable and dubiously trustworthy Virgil.

We did not meet Dante's fearsome white leopard, or the lion, or even the hungry she-wolf. We did encounter their modern counterparts from time to time. Unlike the wild animals who kept their distance, Russian border guards were eager to find us. Around the middle of our journey, powerful flares illuminated the darkness surrounding us. They fired their guns randomly in our direction, while we took shelter behind trees, but mostly in the undergrowth, since it was less than clear where the assault came from. The guards were alerted by our silhouettes outlined against the moonlit sky as we were crossing a mountain ridge.

We thought the moonlight a blessing. It made the treacherous journey more manageable. It made it easier to find a path through the wilderness and to avoid stepping on snakes or branches, or stumbling over rocks and boulders. It helped us move noiselessly in alien territory and avoid marked trails where we would be more easily found and pursued. Jani moved fast and it was difficult to keep up with him and not fall behind. Falling behind more than a few steps meant getting hopelessly lost.

"You don't want to get lost in these parts," Jani instructed us needlessly. I certainly didn't. Robi looked out for me, dragging me up steep slopes by my hand when I could not keep up. He was an experienced mountaineer. Eva had even more trouble. She was not a hiker, was heavy set, pampered, and not used to physical exertion. It did not take long for her to become terrified and miserable, freely sharing her discontent with all of us. It was more than a little demoralizing.

We needed to see but avoid being seen or heard. Not an easy feat as we soon learned. Still, we managed to do so for several hours now, climbing in silence. Branches and shrubs tore our clothes, our arms and legs were bruised by rocks and shrubbery while stumbling down mountain sides. I was getting exhausted, not used to such strenuous hikes. Still we could not stop for more than a few seconds at a time. We had to move fast to get across the border before daylight. Jani thought we were getting closer. I could not imagine how he could tell, as there was only darkness and mountains and wilderness around us. So far, we had been lucky; we had not been seen, or perhaps the menacing towers we skirted were still abandoned. We had managed to cross a couple of open minefields as well.

"These have been cleared recently," Jani said.

I hoped to God he was right. There was no time to be afraid. It is worth it, I kept telling myself. The Promised Land, if not quite Paradise lay just ahead. And I was with Robi. We were together. It gave me hope. He would not do anything really foolish I thought. I was still in the hero worship phase of our relationship.

It was not until we had to cross the next-to-last mountain ridge that the guards detected us from one of the nearby watch towers. Moonlight betrayed us in the end. I filed this away for future reference: helpfulness is a relative concept. What is helpful in one situation can become dangerous under the right, or rather wrong, circumstances...

Still, we were lucky again. We ducked, we ran, we crawled and hid until we found a narrow trail that rolled away from the crest and down the other side of the mountain, hoping we would disappear from sight. We held our breath because the cold air turned it visible as we exhaled. We lay perfectly still on the mountainside under some shrubs, careful not to make a sound. We did not move. Invisible creatures prowled around us and the natural sounds of the wilderness made us cringe. We clung together for what seemed like eternity, until we were reasonably sure that nobody was coming after us. Perhaps it was too cold, perhaps it was too late, perhaps the guards were too sleepy or lazy, or thought they were mistaking some mountain sheep for people. Who knows? We only knew that the flares disappeared and the gunfire stopped. Cautiously, very cautiously, we continued our journey.

It was this incident that must have decided our guide Jani to bail out while the going was good. So, about a half-hour later he led us to another mountain peak. The view was magnificent even in the dark. We made sure we were carefully camouflaged this time, hiding in the shadows of ancient trees. The night was brilliant with stars you wanted to get lost in. Beneath us lay two seemingly identical villages at opposite ends of the valley. Both seemed to be tiny from this distance. They were illuminated by flickering electricity mirroring the blinking stars above. They were positioned at different ends of the Alpine mountain range, separated by extensive farmland and vineyards.

Jani pointed to the right. "That's Hungary. You don't want to go in that direction." He pointed to the left. "That's Austria."

"Good luck," he added as he disappeared completely and so noiselessly that he seemed to melt away without a trace.

"SHIT," said Robi.

"What the Hell?????" was my contribution. "You can't do this to us!" I added feebly addressing the empty space that had once contained Jani.

Jozsi and Eva said nothing. They were out of breath, as they both suffered from asthma. And shock in this case.

We were in the middle of nowhere, surrounded in the night by primordial wilderness, cold, exhausted and quite lost. But we were given a glimpse of freedom, a glimpse of the Promised Land. Provided that Jani wasn't mistaken or lying. I thought of Moses. He too was granted a glimpse of the Promised Land, but was never allowed to enter it. I always thought that was very unfair. Was that going to be our fate as well? Even if we made it, did we have any idea what was waiting on the other side? None, really. Only hopes and fantasies. Not for the first time during that night, I was glad that baby Andrea was at home safe and sound and out of danger. Or so we hoped.

The immediate problem was that we had no way to reach the valley directly. I wished we had a parachute or a glider to sail down to the valley. We had to leave the summit instead and reenter the forest. This meant we lost all visual clues or whatever sense of direction we had individually and collectively. We often ended up going around in circles. I remembered my childhood fairy tales. They were right. It was easy to get lost in the forest. Especially if you were fleeing a monster and had to hide, had to be on high alert to avoid being captured.

Robi came to the rescue as usual. He took charge, he seemed confident. He was an experienced mountaineer, at least around the Buda Hills. He had been trained in night hiking nine years before by the Hanhatz, the Zionist youth organization where we first met. I don't know how confident he actually felt, but we trusted him. We needed a leader. Robi whipped out his trusted compass.

"We are going this way," he announced confidently. He always had on him a compass and a Swiss Army knife. And he always knew the way. The compass may have been part of the Swiss Army knife. It was tiny and we all knew it was not entirely reliable under the circumstances. It was almost impossible to read in the dark, but it was better than nothing. In any case, we had no choice but to get back to the woods and find a path that led down to the valley. Unfortunately, whatever path we chose would meander, as mountain paths will, down and up and sometimes straight on. Eventually we heard a dog bark in the distance and we kept away. We could not tell if it was a German or Hungarian bark. We lost our bearings often as we wondered through the mountains, and we could not be sure where we were. Had we crossed over to Austria by now, or were we approaching a Hungarian village?

After a long, bruising descent to the valley, we found ourselves surrounded by vineyards.

"It seems the vine is tied differently here," I observed.

"Since when were you an expert on vineyards?" Robi sounded

skeptical, but affectionate, so I did not mind. I was used to it. This was not the time to explain that I had wandered around vineyards in and around Siofok and Lake Balaton, where my parents were exiled by the Communists. I kept quiet; this was not the time to argue the point. It was dark in the valley; the moon hid behind the clouds. We were shadows moving cautiously across the landscape. We could not see, but neither could we be seen. The shape and meaning of everything were hidden in the dark. Those lights in the distance could mean danger and defeat, imprisonment, even death, or they could mean freedom and redemption. There was no way of knowing. We were at the end of our strength, beat up, lost, and exhausted.

"I cannot go on," Eva said once again, but this time she meant it. She sat down on the wet ground. "I don't care if we are still in Hungary, I need food and rest. This was a terrible idea. I want to go home!" she was sobbing inconsolably now.

"It was your idea and it was a good idea. Anyway, we cannot go home even if we wanted to, which we don't," said Jozsi. "Shush now, so we won't be discovered. We will rest for a while until we figure out what to do."

Robi still had a small piece of beef jerky in his pocket and he gave it to Eva. There was no water left. We huddled together in the vineyard—cold and tired and scared—trying to make a decision. I looked up at the cloudy sky.

"We need a sign!" I muttered. Robi gave me a hug.

It was then that I spotted something unusual on the ground not too far from us. It did not seem organic like a twig or stone. I decided to move a little closer to get a better look. "It looks like paper, it's all crumpled up. A crumpled newspaper?" I muttered to no one in particular.

This produced some mild interest. Exhaustion has a tendency

to slow the mind. It took a few seconds for the information to sink in. A newspaper would be printed either in German or Hungarian and might give us a clear indication as to where we were. Hopefully. But how to tell in the dark? We had a flashlight, but had dared not use it so far.

"We could use my hat to shield the light," said Robi and proceeded to take off his cap.

Jozsi shone the flashlight under it carefully. I was the only one who didn't need glasses so I was the one to look. Eva did not move. She just sat on the ground semi-comatose.

I touched the thing gingerly and then with growing excitement.

"It is a crumpled page from a newspaper," I called out before bursting into hysterical laughter.

Robi was visibly alarmed.

"No, I am not going off the far edge," I said grinning broadly. "It's just that there is good news and, well, bad news." I could not stop giggling. In fact, I am still giggling now.

Robi grabbed the paper from my hands staring at it.

"The good news is that this is indeed a page from an Austrian newspaper…"

I looked at Robi.

"The bad news is that there are big brown spots all over it as you can see. Smell it! Yes, it definitely stinks! Looks to me like someone was wiping their ass with it…"

I held up the thing for all to see and smell, and we laughed and hugged and jumped up and down and would have hollered but did not think it would be safe yet. Nobody felt tired anymore as we started out in the direction of the village. We must have looked like Dorothy and friends following the Yellow Brick Road in reverse. Except we definitely did not want to go home and there wasn't a road. I still feel pretty confident however, that no one in human history has been as happy and jubilant over finding shit as we were.

It didn't occur to us at the time, but this moment turned out to be a perfect metaphor for some of the mixed blessings that were inevitably waiting us in the early years of our "refugeedom"…

It took us several more hours stumbling across the vineyards in pitch dark, guided only by the cluster of blinking lights in the distance, to reach the outskirts of the village. Suddenly we were surrounded by shadows emerging from the dark.

"Welcome to St. Margarete," a tall, youngish man said in German. He must have seen that we were dazed, apprehensive and disoriented. "You are safe now," he added.

We relaxed. He looked legit, and he spoke German, but doubts lingered. You get a bit paranoid living under a dictatorship. Especially when you are fleeing from a dictatorship. How come they were waiting for us? How did they know we would pop up? Jozsi and I knew some German and we asked.

"We have been on the lookout for refugees every night for the past two weeks. People have been crossing the mountains almost every night. Many don't make it and those who do, like you, need a lot of support. The Red Cross has set up shelters in the schoolhouse. We are volunteers. Our mission is to help you."

I hugged him then, I think we all did. We had felt isolated in Hungary. We thought the whole world had abandoned us. People in St. Margarete cared. Austria cared. A wave of relief swept over us as we entered the schoolhouse. It was warm, a fire burning in the hearth. There were lights everywhere and friendly faces welcomed us in the small hours of the night. It was truly amazing. The smell of bacon, eggs, and warm fresh bread overwhelmed us. Until now we didn't quite realize how hungry we were. And thirsty and dirty.

Disheveled and messy. Our clothes were torn, we were covered with mud, and we had bloody scratches and bruises all over our bodies. We kept on thanking our rescuers, mostly in Hungarian. Tears of relief were abundant. We desperately needed to eat and drink, but we needed to get to a bathroom first. After cleaning up as best we could, we were treated to what seemed to us a feast. Much of this seems blurry now. We were on sensory overload. Exhaustion caught up with us and we were close to collapse.

The small school auditorium was already pretty crowded. It was late at night and people were sleeping on piles of straw. It was the best the village could do. There were no more beds available in private homes. This was a new experience for us, but we were beyond caring. It seemed preferable to sleep on the floor on straw in freedom than to have a down-filled comfortable bed in circumstances that amounted to slavery. Remember, we were young and idealistic. The yearning for freedom can be as intense, as essential, as the need for food and water. This was true for us and for a lot of other people. Then and now.

We settled on a good inch of straw and wrapped ourselves in blankets given us by our rescuers. I snuggled up to Robi, our arms wrapped around each other. It is amazing how cozy you can feel even under the most unlikely circumstances when you are curled up with someone you love radiating warmth and reassurance.

The last thing I remember hearing was a kindly German voice: "There will be a bus early tomorrow morning after breakfast. It will take you to Vienna, to a Refugee Camp where you'll have proper accommodations."

Then I blacked out.

14. On the Other Side of the Fence: Harsh New Beginnings

We never got to Vienna, since the refugee camps there were full. Bursting at the seams. We wound up in Linz, a beautiful ancient town on the shores of the Danube, about twice the size of Columbia, where I live now in Maryland. Linz had a checkered history, like all old towns in that part of the world. Hitler had grown up there and was quite fond of it. He considered Linz his hometown. Mauthausen, which had been a notorious Nazi concentration camp a little over a decade before, was just twelve miles away.

We were blissfully unaware of this as we were deposited at an old allied army base where we were promptly and efficiently fed and "processed" by the Austrian authorities. This was the first of many more vettings to come. Various refugee organizations, mostly faith-based except for the Red Cross, took us under their wings. We were issued blankets and donated clothing. In spite of all the hardships during and after the war, I had never before worn second-hand clothes. Mended and homemade ones, yes, but not hand-me-downs. There was no one to hand things down. I was an only child and there were no other children in our extended family.

I was most grateful for these gifts. The clothes we escaped in were in shreds, unwearable. We received a couple of warm sweaters, a cardigan, sweatshirts, a pair of pants, and jeans. They didn't exactly fit, but there was at least an attempt to approximate our sizes.

I had never seen things like that except in some Western movies. And there was more! I still remember a swirly, shiny, deep-black velvet skirt covered with undulating neon-colored ribbons in electric blue, red, yellow, and lime green. I've never seen anything like it. It was the most glamorous, magical thing I had ever set eyes on. It made me feel like a princess, beautiful and civilized. I ceased to be a homeless, penniless refugee when I wore it. The skirt became my most prized possession for the next two years. This was not all! We were also issued a small voucher to purchase new underwear in town, since hand-me-down underwear was not hygienic. This was an unusual, delicate gesture, we thought.

We had food and water, we had shelter and warm clothes, and we had dreams of a new, better life. Meanwhile, the present was anything but glamorous. Accommodations were crowded, if mostly clean. We were expected to do most of the cleaning and other chores. Only fair, we thought. Communal living had its ups and downs. People squabbled, families fought, children cried. Yes, there were children. I wanted to hold my own child, like other mothers did. I was getting angry with Robi about not letting Andrea come with us. We could have given her a mild sleeping pill, like other parents did, so that she wouldn't cry during the escape. Robi pointed out that I was being unreasonable, since I had agreed to leave her behind. This was true, of course, and I had to admit it. This was the closest we ever got to an argument then and for many years to come. Sixteen years, to be exact. Only much later did I realize how much I resented being presented with this choice and the resulting anguish and anxiety during the period of separation. It seemed to me at the time that he did not fully understand or share the intensity of my distress, although I knew he cared.

In camp we had to stand in line for our meals, for the showers, for practically everything. We had had a lot of experience standing in line in Hungary, for bread, meat and groceries, mostly. Here the lines were orderly, unlike in raucous Budapest. Besides, we certainly had the time. Lots and lots of time. After the nerve-wracking adventure of crossing the border, which required all of our focus and attention, we now had time to contemplate our predicament.

Yes, we had escaped tyranny and we were free in a free world where we could think and say and do whatever we wanted as long as it was not disruptive to camp or immigration policies. We did not have to lie or dissemble to stay alive.

But we were homeless, stateless, penniless refugees, without jobs, far away from our homes and loved ones. Our lives were full of uncertainty. We did not know how long we would be stuck in camp. We didn't have any connections or prospects for being sponsored and resettled as far as we knew. We missed our infant daughter, her cooing, her smile. I missed holding her to my chest, her tiny fingers clutching mine. I even missed her cry. We worried about her well-being and we were terrified that we might not get her back. We also worried about our parents. And we missed our friends. By now many of them had escaped as well, but we did not know where they were. It drove us crazy at times. In retrospect, I think our sanity was saved by recognizing that we were all in the same predicament. The whole camp shared similar stories, and we supported each other.

It helped that we were mostly young and enthusiastic, with endless optimism and boundless energy. Despite our past experiences and thanks to our ignorance, we had no doubt that we would conquer all difficulties and succeed in creating a beautiful new free life! We did have our down times, but they did not last.

We had the moral support of the free world. We were admired and encouraged for resisting and escaping tyranny. People were kind to us, for the most part. Most importantly, we were empowered by a sense of mission. We had a purpose. We firmly believed that we were there to establish a better life for our children. Robi and I were going to rescue Andrea from the prison that was Hungary and give her the opportunities we had never had. We would build ourselves a dignified life in a free society and contribute to its wellbeing. Miraculously, we actually did accomplish all of this and more. It took a lifetime of prolonged struggle.

We were able to laugh even in the most difficult times. We could see and appreciate life as strange and bizarre. We managed not to take ourselves too seriously. It was the gift of our Hungarian-Jewish heritage.

In this respect, Bandi (Andrew) was a gift from heaven. We could always count on him to cheer us up. We met him at the camp. He was there by himself, a tall, dark, handsome, gregarious young man with bushy eyebrows, a booming baritone, and an infectious smile. He was a talented opera singer from Budapest who was a few years older than Robi. The three of us became close friends. Robi and Bandi would burst into song several times during the day and many evenings after dinner. Robi loved to sing in those days, even though he didn't have any formal training. Robi and Bandi were popular not only with the refugees, who were moved to tears by the Hungarian folk songs, but also with our Austrian minders, who enjoyed spirited renditions of arias from the Marriage of Figaro, the Abduction from the Seraglio, and other operas. Mostly Mozart. Bandi's powerful baritone and Robi's seductive tenor enchanted the captive audience...

The two men had fun and temporarily forgot their helpless state while basking in their well-deserved success. Robi also fought boredom by being generally helpful to anyone needing help. He could fix practically anything and things were constantly breaking down and needing to be fixed at the aging and by-now overcrowded camp.

I was lucky. Within days of arriving, I had a job. The camp was short of interpreters. When the administration found out that I spoke German, English, and a smattering of French and Russian, they offered me a job. I would gladly have done it for free, but they insisted on giving me a small stipend. We were then able to get a pass and explore Linz, where we could stop at a nice coffee house, order real freshly brewed coffee without chicory and with Schlag (whipped cream), and share a slice of Linzer Torte. We could pretend to be just normal people like everybody else. I would order in German and the men would smile and talk rapidly in a made-up language, pretending to be tourists from some faraway land. Sometimes it actually worked, and the nice waitress in her pretty fringed apron would ask where we were from. That put me on the spot and I had to improvise. Relying on our nice waitress's presumably limited knowledge of geography (this was 1956, remember?) I would come up with some outlandish answer. That usually did it, since the nice waitress was reluctant to reveal her ignorance of this unknown and unknowable non-existent country. We thought this was a lot of fun then, but I am rather embarrassed thinking about it now…

With my paycheck, we could also buy small necessities, such as a mild fragrant soap, a good toothbrush, and nice-smelling toothpaste. A belt for Robi, new straps for his wristwatch. Things like that. I could not resist, among other things, beautiful silk stockings that were lighter than a spider's web, but a lot more enchanting. They seemed like the most luxurious thing I had ever owned. They were totally useless under the circumstances, and it would be a long time until I wore them.

The greatest morale booster was a brief call to Mami (Robi's mom)—thanks to the International Red Cross—after we had arrived. It took a nerve-wracking week or ten days, which seemed like an eternity. We were allowed only one call. Mami reassured us that Andrea was well and thriving. My mother had picked her up as arranged and taken her to Siofok. The Revolution had hardly touched Siofok, and life there was less chaotic and much safer.

Mami sounded relatively good, happy that we had made it safe and sound. She missed us. She and her mother were safe and well, looked after by her two sisters and brothers-in-law. They did not expect to be harassed much, since they were older, retired, and not a danger to the system. Mami instructed us to take care of ourselves, not to worry, and to under no circumstances return home. Not that we ever seriously considered doing so, but it was good to have her permission and support for staying.

We were somewhat reassured, though profoundly saddened for our country at the same time. We knew from the local papers and news stations that the new Kadar government was capturing and executing freedom fighters as well as the liberal politicians who tried to extricate Hungary from the yoke of the Soviet Bloc. Their goal had been to establish an independent, democratic Hungary patterned after Austria. We already knew from the Western newspapers and radio broadcasts that this attempt had failed. Independence was doomed. Revolution had made a highly visible statement but had not accomplished anything much except for chaos and loss of life. Another reign of terror was settling in for the long haul.

Now we had to make some decisions. What to do next? We couldn't and wouldn't want to stay in camp much longer. Camp counselors asked everyone what country they wanted to settle in. Austria could not take all of us, even if we wanted to stay, and most of us didn't. For Robi and me it was too close to home. Correction.

It was too close to the Soviet Army next door in Hungary. It was also too closely connected to the toxic past. We were Jews and too many Austrians of our parents' generation were personally connected to the Nazis and the persecutions. In 1956, there was no way to tell who was who. Austria and Germany were out of the question, and Switzerland took only a handful of refugees. It would be a very long time before I would feel halfway comfortable staying in a German-speaking country.

Most people in the camp had connections and/or family in one Western country or another. We didn't, or thought we didn't. Robi wanted to go to America, "the land of opportunities," the promised land for an engineer. I had serious problems with this, because of Andrea. I was convinced that distance mattered. I did not want to go any farther away than absolutely necessary from where my daughter now was. Traveling to the other side of the Atlantic would forever keep me from my daughter. I felt it in my bones. This time I stuck to my guns. I refused to go to America. Robi eventually saw the point, especially after it became clear that the United States had a strict quota system and would admit only a few refugees a year. There was a long waiting list. (Sound familiar?) We might have to wait many years without any assurances.

By this time there were over 200,000 of us Hungarians to re-settle. Most of us were young and educated. Not as many as the current Syrian crisis, but the world population was smaller then. Our prospects for getting out of camp were not good, and we needed to get out. In many ways we had less freedom of movement there than back in Hungary. We were treated well, but we were stateless illegal aliens. We needed to find a home. We needed to sign up for asylum in one or more countries on the Continent. Whoever would take us. We needed to find a sponsor. We needed to get on with it.

One day I was called away from work and told to go to the camp office. Had I done something wrong? No, I had a telephone call. I was incredulous. This must be a mistake. We did not know a soul in Austria or anywhere else in Europe for that matter. Calls from Hungary were rare and had to be prearranged. Was something wrong at home? Was Andrea OK? Was this an emergency call? By the time I got to the office I had managed to work myself into panic.

"You have a call from England," the woman behind the desk informed me. "We didn't know you had connections in England," she said, looking at me accusingly. I gave her an apologetic smile and grabbed the phone. It was my cousin Magdi. I had last seen Magdi when I was five and she was twelve. It was then that her family had left Budapest for London, just a day or two before the war began.

Communication with the West had been non-existent for over four years during WWII and blacked out in Hungary during the Communist regime. Letters that somehow managed to get through were heavily censored. Our families had lost touch. There was a brief contact in 1945 when the War ended. We knew that Magdi's father, my uncle, had died. Zoli, my youngest uncle, was supposed to relocate to England and take care of the children, Magdi and Imre. Then the borders closed and he never made it out. The families lost contact, seemingly permanently.

I had only vague memories of Magdi, mostly that she loved me and played with me like an older sister when I was very young. I had vaguely loving feelings toward her but her memory was submerged in the opaque impenetrable past.

Now she had tracked us down via the Red Cross.

"Thank God we found you! Where are you? Are you all right?" The words came tumbling out, barely coherent, high pitched with worry and excitement. There was a lot more, but I could understand only fragments, partly because of my own excitement, and partly because she spoke in rapid English. British English, not a word of Hungarian.

We were under a fairly stringent time limit, since overseas calls were expensive. I gathered that she was living in Brighton with her husband and five-year-old son, John. Imre, my younger cousin, was in London, a young man about town. They wanted us to come to England. She would sponsor us. We cried and hugged over the phone and tried to catch up with each other's lives. I was profoundly moved and awed by this sudden gift of a new family and a new home. It was totally unexpected. We exchanged basic information and promised to keep in touch.

I practically flew to find Robi. "You won't believe what happened! Magdi called!"

He gave me a blank look. "Who?"

Of course, they had never met and Robi barely knew she existed.

I explained. We had a place to go now. "She will sponsor us and I love England. I admire them. I have always dreamt of going there. We wouldn't be too far away from Andrea and the Brits will help us get her back," I added with typical optimism.

Robi looked dubious at first, but eventually got caught up in my excitement. We needed to get out of camp and here was the perfect opportunity. The next day we applied for a visa and resettlement in England.

ENGLAND

15. Exiting the Continent

For the next few weeks we were caught up in a whirlwind of activities— official interviews, filling out documents, filling out more documents, and answering increasingly arcane questions proving that we were who we said we were, that we had no criminal records, etc. Fair enough. England needed to know that we were OK people deserving asylum. The UK had a strict quota, but Magdi's sponsorship advanced us to near the top of the line. Robi's engineering degree and experience were also a plus, as was my relative fluency in the English language.

After all this was checked out, recorded, stamped, verified and approved by all concerned, we were finally ready to go. We said our goodbyes to our new and old friends at the Refugee Camp, especially Jozsi and Eva, the couple we escaped with. They were hoping to get to the U.S., where Eva had family connections. Most of the refugees wanted to go to "America." It was considered something of a "Promised Land," despite its strict quota system for accepting refugees. This meant a much longer wait before they could leave. Bandi, our opera singer friend, was also heading for England, which was a good thing. His gregarious good nature and high energy kept both of us mobilized and happy. We were positively brimming with cheer, excitement, and unrealistic expectations. It would be reasonable to assume that we would worry about the unknown future in an unknown land, but I honestly don't remember any worries. We were too caught up in the adventure. Furthermore, we could not even begin to attempt to get our daughter back until we had settled somewhere on this globe, until we had at least an address, a home. Underlying our every move, every single day, was the awareness that we did not have our baby with us.

"You know she is safe and happy with your parents. You talked to them. She is well loved, even adored, and probably spoiled rotten. You know how well they take care of her! She is much better off with them than in this crowded refugee camp," Robi kept on saying whenever he saw me brooding. Usually after helping other moms, comforting their crying infants, cuddling them, feeling the comfort of their warmth, their smiles.

"Robi is right," I kept telling myself, "we are doing this even more for her then for ourselves. We do not want her to grow up the way we did. We want a better, safer future for her."

This made a lot of sense, but I still had an aching void when I looked at other children. I still felt it was wrong to leave her behind. I did not know when or how I would get her back; I only knew that I would do so, and I would never let her go again. We tried not to talk about it, not to think about it too much, for it was too scary, too painful. In retrospect, I am not sure we were ready for England, or that England was altogether ready for us, although this did not occur to me until much later.

We were an undifferentiated mess of garrulous ignorance, good will, and enthusiasm. Not altogether bad, as it allowed us to stay largely unaware of, or at least underestimate, the inevitable difficulties we were about to face resettling in a new country and adapting to a culture and social structure that could not be any more different from our native one. In our innocence, we expected to be welcomed with open arms, appreciated, and loved by all for our courage to escape oppression and embrace freedom.

In all fairness, this is what happened most of the time, but we also occasionally encountered the defensive resentment and mistrust that immigrants have faced everywhere, throughout history. Very few have escaped the mixed undercurrents of the refugee experience, from time immemorial. We were aware that to some extent we would always be "strangers in a strange land," even in the Promised Land...

We soon learned that being a refugee was one step down from being an immigrant, and being an immigrant was a far cry from being a citizen, even when you became a citizen eventually. This was nothing new to us. Being a Jew prepared us for this. Being a Jew prepares you to be regarded by some, or many, as an outsider, even in your own country. Except that this was not our own country. Here we were truly outsiders, so it was easier to accept it. We hoped, indeed we were convinced, that with time, all this would change and one day we would wake up and know that we truly belonged.

16. Arrival

Our New Life started with a plane ride. Definitely a "first." Was I apprehensive? Of course I was. I had never ridden in a plane, only dreamt about it. I was too excited to be afraid. Robi explained that this was a two-engine prop plane, the kind the Brits used in WWII. I seem to remember that it was a military transport, but I am not quite sure. I must have been in an altered state of consciousness, immersed in the unfamiliar, magical sensation of flying. Sailing through the air. In a box. Transported across the continent and the Channel in a matter of hours. It seemed unnatural, surreal. All I remember is that we landed somewhere in England and it wasn't Heathrow. It might have been Lakenheath or another military base; I am not sure. I felt tremendous relief. We had finally left the Continent, the scene of so much carnage and personal suffering. I did not know yet that suffering is everywhere and you cannot run away from it.

After landing and the initial "processing," consisting of checking our temporary Austrian IDs and British visas, we were piled into buses. I loved those buses. They were small and clean and boxy with big windows. It was dark by then and all I could see were the skeletal outlines of windswept trees darkly guarding the road, illuminated by the occasional lights of distant communities visible from the narrow winding roads. We traveled at what seemed to me a reckless speed. Rain drummed on the roof of the bus and the rhythmic swish of the windshield wipers created a hypnotic rhythm. I felt relaxed and well-protected. Exhausted, but safe, perhaps for the first time in my life. I did not know where I was, or where I was going, but it did not matter. I was with Robi and felt that I was arriving in a magical new home. Well, not quite. As it turned out the next day, we were taken to a processing facility for refugees in Aldershot, Hampshire, a POW camp during WWII. We were housed comfortably, dormitory style. We were told that there would be debriefings, and I began to worry if my English would be good enough for that. And how about Robi and Bandi? They did not speak any English at all.

I needn't have worried. The next day, after a stupefyingly lavish English breakfast of three rashers of bacon, two eggs, sausages, oatmeal, and toast and jelly, the individual interviews began. I was ushered into a small, nondescript office, more like a cubicle with walls. It had a metal desk and a couple of chairs. A pleasant, clean-shaven young man in a business suit stood up and greeted me in flawless Hungarian. I was astonished. In my experience, no one who was not Hungarian spoke Hungarian. They simply didn't, ever. My interviewer was clearly British and looked like an Oxford graduate, a Malcolm Lowry or Graham Greene type. I don't remember his name. It probably wasn't his name anyway. Let's call him Mr. Y. He was friendly, personable and put me instantly at ease. Mr. Y was very well informed about Hungarian affairs and history, both past and present. He was familiar with the literature and the culture. I was impressed. I trusted him. He reminded me of my old English teacher back in Hungary, who had disappeared mysteriously shortly after the Communist takeover, only to reappear briefly just at the time of the Revolution. He had claimed not to speak any Hungarian, but I never believed him.

I actually enjoyed the interview. I was eager to talk about my experiences, to share them with someone who could not have possibly experienced anything remotely like it in their protected, peaceful life. Or so I thought. In retrospect, he was probably from the Home Office or MI-5 with the mission to screen refugees and identify "undesirables." He was highly skilled, respectful and I never felt like I was being interrogated. Not that I needed to be interrogated. I was eager to give as much information about the pitiful state of Hungary as I could. It was important that the West knew! Surely they would do something about it, surely they would help, I thought.

"Why did you not come and help the Revolution?" I asked Mr. Y. "We were fighting for democracy. The BBC encouraged us."

"So did Voice of America," Mr. Y said smiling. I didn't.

"We couldn't," he said and stopped smiling. "We had the Suez crisis on our hands and many other problems. It was bad timing. I am sorry," he added. "We will do what we can now to help you, and everyone who escaped, to start a new life of freedom."

"I will need your help to get my baby girl back. I need to get her out of Hungary," I told him.

He looked at me, startled. "You have a child? Tell me more about her. Where is she?"

I told him all about it and he made many notes.

"We cannot get her out of Hungary, but we will support you every way we can. We will grant her a visa, but you need to find a way to get her here," he said and gave me his card.

I believed him. "Thank you. We will work hard; we will do our best. We are grateful for your support. I promise you, we won't be a burden," I assured him. I felt like hugging him, but we shook hands instead. Brits are not into hugging. Especially not then.

We did not know what the future would hold, but we were full of youthful hope and an inner certainty that everything would work out somehow. It turned out that Mr. Y was as good as his word and delivered on his promise when the time came.

Although hastily improvised to accommodate the influx of Hungarian refugees, the process was quite efficient. In a few days both of us were cleared and discharged. We parted from Bandi only to meet up again later when we moved to London.

Cousin Imre volunteered to pick us up and take us to Magdi's house in Brighton. We may have been cousins, but we were also complete strangers to each other. We had neither spoken nor seen each other since we were five. I had not even had a photo to send him for identification purposes. I immediately recognized him as his tall skinny frame unfolded from the small car he drove. He looked so much like the younger version of my father and uncles. Hugging was not easy as he was towering over me, but we hugged anyway. That's all it took for us to become connected, to become family. Imre did not speak a word of Hungarian. He had a public school accent, which sounded great, but was hard to understand. Not quite as hard as understanding cockney, the language of the street, but a close runner-up.

It was then that I experienced the first profound and fundamental loss resulting from our decision to leave. We were prepared to give up our parents, our friends, our homes, our professions, our way of living, even our child, at least temporarily. All that we foresaw and expected. But I had never thought about losing my language, the unique and glorious Hungarian language. Language determines the way we think, the way we reason, the way we grieve, the way we love, the way we tell jokes, the way we communicate, the way we see the world. I realized in that moment that most of who I was was tied to the language I spoke, the language I thought in. From birth to age twenty-two to this very moment, I had lived a Hungarian reality and now I had to learn to change over and enter a different reality circumscribed by another language. In Austria, in the refugee camp, we all spoke Hungarian, except for our minders, the people who took care of us. But here in England even my family could not understand me unless I spoke English. The impact was profound, an instantaneous divide. I knew with absolute certainty that I must bridge this divide if I didn't want to become a "stranger in a strange land" for the rest of my life. I sensed that you can't serve two masters in these matters. In retrospect the ongoing struggle to think in English, to master the language as though I had been born into it, began in that moment and is still ongoing.

It was time to get into the car with Imre, time to begin a new life in a new country, alongside a newly discovered family. We didn't have many belongings, just one small suitcase each, filled with a motley selection of secondhand clothing gifted to us by the Red Cross and HIAS (a Jewish charity). During the exodus of 200,000 Hungarians fleeing their country, religious charities mobilized worldwide and took up collections to help as many refugees as they could.

I was wondering how we would all fit in the tiny car. We soon learned that most cars were very small in England, since gasoline, or petrol as the Brits call it, was still scarce and at a premium eleven years after the War ended. The current fighting over the Suez Canal didn't help much either. Robi was 6'1", not quite as tall as Imre but close to it. The two men sat in front and I curled up with the luggage in the back. I made myself as small as I could, which wasn't very difficult as I was not quite 5'4" and I did not weigh all that much in those days. Odds and ends, including sandwiches, were tucked in the tiny trunk, or "boot" as Imre called it. We never went anywhere without food since the war ended, a habit that still holds.

17. Rottingdean

It has been over sixty years since we arrived at Magdi's house in Rottingdean, then a poor suburb of Brighton in Sussex some forty-five miles out of London. Even today, it is difficult to sort out my thoughts and feelings about those events. The differences between expectations and reality were so shattering and confusing that they simply had to be ignored for the time being, in order to go on. I suspect that this is the case for most refugees even today. Yet, I should have been better prepared than most. I spoke the language reasonably well, I was familiar with the history and literature of England, and I loved and respected the culture. My cousins had grown up here and considered themselves English. I thought I knew everything I needed to know about them, but in reality, I knew nothing. I knew absolutely nothing about Magdi's or Imre's personal lives, about the extent of their or their country's collective trauma during WWII, about the heroic, difficult recovery that was still ongoing. I was immersed in our own sufferings and it was comforting to imagine that the West, specifically England, was a place of peace and prosperity, an ideal society, a Utopia just waiting to embrace us with compassion and love.

Brighton itself is a popular, upscale resort town in Sussex with good train service, less than fifty miles away from London. Many Londoners who had not yet been able to restore their bombed-out residences in the city lived there at the time. It is a beautiful place, perched on top of the cliffs overlooking the restless, stormy Atlantic.

It has two universities and eccentric and extravagant architecture, such as the Royal Pavilion built in the 19th century by the Prince of Wales. Today it is considered the "happiest town in Britain" by some. I don't think it was the happiest town then, and Rottingdean was even less so. (It has an inauspicious name for a village, which is perhaps why I had forgotten it until Imre reminded me today. He called from London as I was writing this and I questioned him about his memories of that day sixty years ago. Actually, the name has nothing to do with rotting, it means "the people of Rota" in old Saxon. Obviously, it goes back a long way, like most things in Britain.)

Anyway, Magdi's rented house was far from upscale. She lived there with Jack, her husband, and little John, their five-year-old son. I remember it as a small, jerry-built, cluttered "bungalow" with two tiny bedrooms, all on one level. It had a very basic kitchen and a bath in addition to the living room. The whole thing was probably no more than eight- to nine-hundred square feet, not unusual for England, where small living spaces predominate.

Magdi welcomed us enthusiastically with all the warmth and love of an older sister. Imre just dropped us off and left hurriedly with promises to see us soon. Even in my distracted state, I noticed that their relationship appeared to be strained. It certainly was, as I found out later.

What do you do when you see your cousin after twenty years, for the first time in your adult life? There is of course always hugging. And we did hug and we did cry. Robi was included in this primal bonding process, but I could sense his bewilderment and unease since he did not understand a word we said. Jack was nowhere to be seen—he was out of town—and little John did not seem to have a clue as to what was going on. He looked skittish about the onslaught of strangers invading his limited space. He looked so small, sweet, anxious and vulnerable, all at the same time. I had the urge to hug him and after some hesitation he allowed me to do so.

"This is wonderful. He is generally not a hugger," said Magdi, obviously pleased.

Further communication was temporarily limited, partly because John appeared to be on the withdrawn side and not particularly chatty, and partly because I could not understand him. Have you ever noticed how hard it is to understand children in a foreign language? It is often hard to understand them even in your own.

Magdi and I surveyed each other.

"You look just like you did when I last saw you at age five," Magdi said. I doubted that very much and told her so.

"I remember, you always played with me and I loved that," I countered. "You were the Big Sister I never had. You were twelve?"

"I was thirteen when we left and I remember we had fun together. I always felt welcomed by your mom and dad. I often felt more comfortable with them than at home. My stepmother didn't care for me you know, particularly after Imre was born." I could not miss the sadness in Magdi's voice. Resentment too.

She was now twenty-nine or so, a tall well-built woman with a bony face, her brooding eyes shining with quick intelligence and caring. Her dark hair was cut in an untidy bob. She was not pretty by a long shot, with her slightly protruding lips and helter-skelter teeth, but she was beautiful in an intangible way and I was drawn to her immediately, connected and grateful. I realized how little I knew about her. It was like having read the beginning of a book and picking it up again a few hundred pages on. I had simply missed out on most of the narrative leading up to the present. There was a lot of catching up to do.

"You cared enough to find us, you plucked us out of the Camp and sponsored us, and you are helping us launch a new life, even though you yourself are not exactly carefree. We are very, very grateful," I told Magdi a few days later, when it was becoming clear that her financial situation wasn't exactly rosy.

Jack, the hitherto-absent husband, was a traveling salesman selling God knows what to whoever would buy it, bringing in sporadic income. He came home briefly a week or so later, a very tall, heavy-set man with blazing blue eyes. We suspected that he wasn't entirely happy to see all these new relatives invading his space. I felt increasing tension in the air. We found out later that it had probably more to do with a difficult marriage than with us being there.

Soon we had short but effective lessons on currency, shopping, weights, and distances. We had been brought up in the metric system and England at the time was not. Learning the currency was especially difficult. I got dizzy just thinking about how many shillings were in a pound and what a halfpenny (haepenny) was. Shillings were solid silver and weighed a ton, as did pennies, which were huge and copper. By contrast the sixpence was a tiny little silver disc, the size of a dime. Distances were measured in miles and yards and inches, temperatures measured in Fahrenheit, not Celsius. Strange concepts for people brought up in the metric system. All this made me feel as though I was living inside a Dickens novel. *Bleak House* came to mind and on good days *Great Expectations.*

Magdi taught us about using public transportation. It was highly developed, but very complex, and for us potentially deadly. Brits drove on the left side of the road! We were not prepared for this for some reason. It meant that we were prime candidates for becoming roadkill, because we kept looking for oncoming traffic on the wrong side. A very, very dangerous practice in London.

We were determined to find jobs and have our own place as

soon as possible. That meant London. There were no jobs in Brighton. Magdi drove us the first couple of times, but after that, we were on our own. She had a part-time job and had to care for John. We would take the bus to London and take the "Tube" (underground) to get around once there. By the time we got to the equivalent of an unemployment office, locals had already taken most of the more promising leads. We knew we had to find a place in London soon. An almost impossible proposition on the small allowance we were given by the government until we found work. And time was not on our side.

Our first glimpse of London was absolutely awesome. For me, it was unimaginably, overwhelmingly huge. I felt dwarfed, crushed by the physical scale of everything. The buildings, the avenues, the distances. I felt small and insignificant like Gulliver in the land of the Giants. Yet it was all very beautiful. I burst out crying in Hyde Park listening to an impassioned speech about some improbable political theory. The speaker had a long beard, disheveled hair and sounded quite angry. A small, good-natured crowd gathered, alternately cheering and booing him. An older man challenged one of his arguments. A lively debate ensued. Nobody cursed, nobody was sworn at or called an idiot, or "the enemy of the people." It was all quite civilized. Nevertheless, I was looking around anxiously for the police to show up and make arrests. All I saw were a couple of bobbies wondering around the park peacefully, completely unconcerned. They didn't even carry a gun! I could only detect a rubber stick dangling cheerfully from their waist. I soon saw that Hyde Park was full of similar speakers on any imaginable subject, however esoteric.

"If you wanted to talk, you found a spot, and some people would always stop and listen," Magdi later explained. "You can try it yourself," she added.

I was horrified at the idea. I could just see the headlines: "Female Refugee Arrested in Hyde Park Agitating in some Incomprehensible Language."

Hyde Park was my first introduction to a working democracy. When the Brits said Free Speech, they meant free speech. For everyone. The internet had not yet been invented, and there was no social media, but there was Hyde Park. Eat your heart out, Twitter!

18. Moving On

Westernfound a room in Earls Court in the heart of the city, practically next to Kensington. Like most things in London, Earls Court dates back at least two thousand years. Today it is an upscale gentrified area, boasting past residents like Alfred Hitchcock and Princess Diana (before she became a Princess, of course). In 1956, it was definitely down-at-the-heels. A fascinating landscape filled with an amazing variety of humanity. A dizzying mixture of immigrants and the favorite hangout of the gay population. A poor man's Soho, before Soho became Soho. Eastern Europeans, Asians, Australians, and Africans mixed amiably with a flamboyantly gay population. It was by no means a "respectable" area, but it was cheap and infinitely entertaining. Up until then I had never seen anything even remotely like it. Every outing was an adventure. I still remember walking down the crowded high street as a beautiful young man emerged around a corner sporting long wavy hair and a small grinning monkey on his shoulder. His companion carried a sleek Siamese cat. Clearly, exotic pets were the thing, including friendly pythons and the like. Nobody gave them a second glance. Anything went in Earls Court in those days. After some initial gaping, we relaxed and enjoyed the scene. Here we ceased to be weird Hungarian refugees. Here everyone was weirder than we were. We ceased to stand out. We fit in.

When I said we rented "a room," I meant just that. A "furnished" room you could hardly turn around in. More like a cell than a room, really. It had a snug bed with a ratty, sagging mattress, a stand with a wash basin and a jug of water for washing up, a small nightstand, and a tiny chest of drawers. I don't remember a window, but there was a single bulb overhead glowing faintly. There was a communal bathroom on each floor with a shower fed by an instant heater. You had to feed it with shillings. When you ran out of shillings, the water turned cold. Very cold. Showering in cold water may be good for the soul, but I found it highly unpleasant and painful. We had a gas heater in our room that also required shillings to operate. No shillings, no heat. Consequently, we were often very cold, but we did our best to keep each other warm. In any case we did not intend to stay there for long. Once we got a job, we could move out, and now, at last, we were in a good position to find one. We were in the heart of town, close to everything.

We turned up at the "unemployment office" early every morning, picking up vacancies, filling out questionnaires, tracking down leads. There were lists of employers, both government agencies and private business owners, who were interested in hiring refugees. Finding our way to job interviews was a good way to get to know the complicated geography of this ancient but modern metropolis and learn how to get around by foot and public transit. Naturally, we could not afford cabs.

Job seeking was a humbling experience. I soon realized I had very little to offer in this strange new world, except for my enthusiasm, willingness to learn, and some language skills. Not that Hungarian was in much demand. In fact, it was not in any demand at all. Neither was there any demand for German—the British were still wary of Germans in 1956—and my French and Russian were not up to par. My relative fluency in English saved me, heavily accented as it was. After several weeks of painful interviews, I got a job with

London Transport, the government agency responsible for running and maintaining all public transit systems in England, such as trains, buses, and subways. We were ecstatic. Well, sort of. It was a government job, secure, and the pay was good, it felt like a fortune to us. The offices were in Westminster around St. James Park, walking distance from the Royal Gardens and Buckingham Palace. Easy to get to, easy to enjoy the beauty of the city. The only problem was the work. After extensive testing, the powers-that-be decided that I had great aptitude for numbers and therefore they put me in the finance department to calculate wages and issue checks accordingly.

I may have had a hitherto unexpected aptitude for numbers, but I sure disliked them. I did not like to count things. I was interested in specifics. In individual characters and events. I wanted to know how things looked, felt, smelled, and tasted. Numbers don't tell you those things. Now here I was busy figuring out worker's wages in an unfamiliar non-metric currency based on how many miles or yards of line repair was recorded, or the amount of weight transported based on measurements like pounds, stones, and other unfamiliar "Imperial measurements," a far cry from the decimal metric system I had grown up with. All this using antiquated office calculators resembling hefty cash registers. Computers or electronic calculators had not even been dreamed of. It helped somewhat that I could do addition and multiplication in my head, thanks to my mother's merciless drilling, but division required pencil and paper or the machines. I was very grateful for the job, but it was a mind-numbing nightmare.

Well, at least not for very long. Once I mastered basic skills, I could enjoy the leisurely pace between payroll times. And it was leisurely. Nobody showed up before 8:30 a.m. and we took our time to settle in. This meant some friendly chatter about the quality of last night's sleep, kids, dates, the news. We organized and coordinated the day's tasks, setting up calculating machines and other equipment, and began some serious work. By 11 a.m., distant chimes signaled the approach of the Trolley and we all dropped what we were doing. It was morning tea time. The Trolley was replete with weak coffee, Tetley's tea, biscuits, jelly, and clotted cream, all for a few pennies. They were dispensed by an elderly woman with wispy white hair, eclectic clothing, and a friendly, chatty disposition. It took me a while to understand what she was saying, being new to cockney, but it didn't really matter. All I had to do was smile, point to things, hand over money and nod occasionally. I was later convinced that Carole Burnett modeled her famous char lady after ours pretty accurately. I quickly learned that I did not need to worry about breakfast at home.

Lunch break came around 1:00 p.m. We ate cucumber or spam sandwiches, or ham or chicken salad. When it did not rain, we snuck out to nearby St. James Park and picnicked under the ancient trees, or walked around enjoying the rare sun, the pelicans, crows, woodpeckers, and the fearless squirrels. We fed the ubiquitous pigeons. We returned to work about forty-five minutes later until afternoon teatime, when the Trolley showed up once again and we dropped everything. We left work around 5:30 or 6:00 p.m., depending on our schedules. All in all, I don't think that we were expected to do more than five hours of work, except for the week before payroll was due, when it became very hectic. Otherwise, it was all very civilized and a total revelation to me. Back home in Hungary, the Communists depicted the Capitalist World as darkly exploitative, with inhuman working conditions of Dickensian proportions. I was aware that we as government workers were somewhat privileged, but it soon became clear that the work ethic was very different here in the West. Workers were protected by laws and labour organizations and powerful trade unions, unlike back in the so-called "socialist" countries.

After a few months at London Transport, I began to feel reasonably comfortable. I did not exactly fit in, but people were kind and made allowances for my heavy accent, my wide-eyed ignorance about how things worked in their country, about my "foreignness." I did not make friends and nobody invited me to their homes, but no one made me feel unwelcome either. Just different. It began to dawn on me, that for now, perhaps this was the best we could hope for in our host country, probably in any host country. It was hard to accept. I so much wanted to belong.

In the meantime, Robi spent his days pounding the pavement looking for a job. We lived very frugally on my salary, saving as much as we could for an apartment to prepare for Andrea's arrival. We did not know when that would happen, but we wanted to be ready. We could save very little, and Robi needed a job. Not only for the money. It was very hard on him not to be the primary breadwinner. It was demoralizing. He also missed the work. He was passionate about it.

He would often come and pick me up after work, and we would explore the city. For dinner we returned to Earls Court. Eating out on a regular basis was beyond our means. With no cooking facilities, we were usually limited to sandwiches. We did have a tiny icebox in the room for milk, butter, and the occasional luxury of cold cuts. Our staple diet consisted of canned foods, such as soups, sardines, tuna, and spam which were a great deal more affordable. There was a shelf that served as a cupboard for tea, sugar, bread and jelly, salt and pepper, paper plates, napkins, and eating utensils. We also had a kettle. We always had some fresh fruit around. I could never get enough of oranges and tangerines, even lemons. They were rare in Hungary back then. We loved bananas; they were filling and so very portable. Perfect for a lunch on the run.

On weekends, especially after paydays, we treated ourselves to breakfast at one of the Lyon's Tea Rooms. Our favorite was on Piccadilly. Lyon's was established in 1894 and renovated in the 1920s by a distinguished interior decorator. It was spacious and beautiful. It reminded us of the New York Cafe in Budapest, or the Gerbaud, a famous patisserie "back home." Prices were quite moderate and they served a lavish English breakfast with eggs, bacon, sausages, scrapple, and biscuits with clotted cream and strawberry and peach preserves. Enough food for us for a whole day. They were also famous for their ice cream. Word has it that Margaret Thatcher worked at Lyon's and helped to develop an improved method of preservation as a chemist before she became a barrister and eventually Prime Minister. It was also there, by default, that we first began to learn about and appreciate the subtleties of good tea, in spite of being then as now, first and foremost coffee people. It happened by default, because back in those days English coffee was weak and watery and without much flavor. Not unlike English cooking, as we later discovered. Magdi, like most of middle-class England at the time, was fond of "one pot cooking." This consisted of a big pot equipped with two or sometimes three levels. A little bit of meat would go in the bottom, and the second level was a strainer, containing root vegetables like potatoes, turnips, carrots that fit seamlessly over it. The top layer, when needed, had veggies that required less cooking, such as mushrooms, parsley, etc. The whole thing would have some broth poured over it, or sometimes just water. After a considerable amount of cooking it was all put on a plate and you had a meal. Hardly any washing up to do and not particularly labor intensive. Pretty neat, if not particularly tasty. English cooking has come a very long way since then, as have English restaurants. In any case, it was a long time before we formed a realistic view about the dietary habits of our host country. At this point we were simply grateful for plentiful food surrounding us.

Most evenings after dinner we sat down to a tutorial. Robi would memorize between 300 and 500 words a day from the English-Hungarian Dictionary we somehow got hold of. I was assigned the task of quizzing him. He would make a list of the words he had studied. I would then read either the English or the Hungarian version in sequence and he would supply the corresponding translation. Once he got them straight, I would quiz him randomly from the list. Actually, Robi picked words alphabetically, if I recall, but we soon realized that this was not practical. The English language has a truly awesome vocabulary. The Oxford English Dictionary has in excess of 59 million words and, according to them, it would take a person 120 years to learn them all. Not that anyone alive does.

Pretty soon we devised a different approach. Robi would list the words he did not understand during the day, during interviews, in the stores, in the headlines of the paper, or on application forms. He memorized all of them and we would practice them in the evening. It was actually fun, though pretty daunting for him I assume. He did not complain. It was a challenge and Robi liked challenges. He still does. For me, it was a challenge in a different way. It certainly helped me improve my English, and it taught me to be more patient and understanding. I was far from an ideal teacher. My accent was almost, though not quite, as bad as Robi's, yet I had the task of "correcting" him when his pronunciation was unintelligible even for me. The phonetic notations in the dictionary were of some help, but not all that much. It was truly the blind leading the sightless. I still have to laugh when I think of it. It helped me realize the infinite challenges of English grammar and pronunciation. I fully shared the general perception of students of the language. It is an extreme challenge to master it. Once you learn the basic framework, you soon find out that the exceptions seem more frequent than the rules. As though a bunch of headstrong children decided the "hell with the rules, we will change things around, do what we want and have fun with it." Perhaps that is one reason for its greatness, the main reason why I have always loved it, cherishing its rebellious mutability…

I was in awe of Robi's feats of memory, focus, drive and determination to master the language. He was used to excelling in whatever he did and he continued to do so. Soon Robi's English improved enough to get a job: an engineering job with a respected firm in London. It was a Junior Engineering job in the Chimney Design Section. England was and still is big on chimneys. Do you remember the film Mary Poppins? The wonderful, magical scene where Dick Van Dyke dances around the tall triple-storied chimneys across the London rooftops with his fellow chimney sweeps? The whole country was and still is full of those. Many of them were crumbling, either damaged during the War or in need of modernization and repair. New ones were being built constantly. It was a growth industry and here to stay. Not terribly exciting, but guaranteed job security. There was even a chance, he was assured, that in due time he could graduate to designing industrial chimneys!

Alas, this was hardly

Robi posing as a tourist in front of Big Ben.

what Robi wanted. It failed to excite him or provide a challenge, but he was always a realist. He did not like the work, but accepted it, at least for now. He knew that it brought us a step closer to providing a new home for our child. He gave up his dream of creating bridges spanning mighty rivers and lakes, said goodbye to visions of cutting-edge steel and concrete structures like those he was designing in Hungary. But only temporarily. For now, he was prepared to master the finer points of good old brick-and- mortar chimney design that have changed very little in a hundred years or so.

It was fortunate that we had both learned the eight fundamental rules of being an immigrant.

- Appreciate what the host country has to offer.
- Accept, for now, being low man/woman on the totem pole.
- Be prepared for starting a new life, including a career, from scratch (for me this was old hat).
- Avoid comparisons with your native country when they are unflattering.
- Remember why you chose to leave your native culture in the first place, and accept, respect and embrace your new environment with all its peculiarities. And believe me, the English have an abundance of peculiarities, bless them all.
- Don't cling to the past or feel entitled to special treatment because of your privations, education, intelligence, or past accomplishments.
- Avoid at all costs feeling superior or unappreciated.
- Above all else, STAY FLEXIBLE.

We learned these things, and much more, through our own mistakes and by observing our emigre community. We saw the pitfalls that made people cranky, miserable, resentful, and resented in turn.

19. Preparations

With two regular—if quite limited—incomes, we could now look for a place that could accommodate a small family, where we could bring our child. I hoped it would be a "permanent" residence. As it turned out we did not have anything close to a permanent residence for the next several decades.

We found a house around March or so, or rather the house found us. Robi was very good at networking and successfully connected with the "old Hungarian" emigrant community. They were people who did what my Uncle Laszlo did, and left Hungary either before WWII or immediately after the war ended in 1945. We did not have much in common. Most of them belonged to our parents' generation and were by now well established in England, often highly successful professionals and businessmen. By and large they seemed a highly conservative, pragmatic community. Some of them were prepared to provide some limited support to us newcomers, especially if there was some benefit to them. Perfectly understandable to my present self, if rather disappointing to my young, idealistic persona.

In any case, we were offered a year lease on a house in Wimbledon Park at a reasonable rent we could afford, as long as we cleaned it up and restored it to its earlier habitable state. Robi even negotiated the first month rent free and no deposit. It was a good thing, since we didn't yet have any money to deposit. We were ecstatic and very grateful. A single-family house all to ourselves! This was unheard of. Wimbledon Park was a good suburban address, even if it was the last stop on the District Line. Easy access to the city, to work. We agreed to the conditions and signed on the dotted line sight unseen, or so I remember. If Robi was more circumspect and saw the house, he was not telling.

Our enthusiasm was considerably dampened, though not altogether extinguished, after our first visit. The place was a disaster area. The house looked OK from a distance; it even had a small front yard as well as some faded grassy space in the back. As you got closer, though, you were hit by an overpowering stench. It wasn't a rotten garbage stench, although the backyard was strewn with cat and dog droppings. It was more like burnt grease mixed with strong curry and other unidentifiable spices. The stench emanated from the kitchen and was deeply ingrained in the walls and floors. For decades afterward, I could not get near an Indian restaurant because it reminded me of that overpowering experience. (I love Indian food now, sixty years later.) It turned out that the large and ever-expanding Pakistani family who used to live there became overwhelmed with small kids, work, housekeeping, and providing shelter for new arrivals. They were not able to pay the rent and ended up trashing the place. Eventually the landlord had to evict them.

We set to work. Whatever practical experience I had with housekeeping was supplemented by past observations back home in the old country. Fortunately, I had strong instincts for good hygiene, and more importantly I knew what it was supposed to look like. So did Robi and Bandi, our friend from the Refugee Camp in Austria, who joined us for this project. After all, the house was big enough for all of us once it became habitable.

We all "girded our loins" as it were, which in my case meant tying a kerchief around my head to protect my hair and donning one of Robi's more ratty donated shirts. The men rolled up their sleeves. We opened all the windows, many of them stuck and requiring a lot of muscle to function. After hauling out the accumulated trash and broken furniture strewn all around the house we started with the kitchen and bathroom. The walls had to be washed with bleach and disinfectant. It took forever to get rid of the burnt-on grease splattered everywhere, especially on the gas stove and the unimaginably filthy sink stained a multitude of colors like a rainbow from Hell. Once done, we moved on to the rest of the house. We had hardly any cleaning equipment except for an old beat-up Hoover (as all vacuum cleaners were called) that worked on and off, but never very efficiently. We had to improvise. It took us several weeks to make the place semi-habitable, working evenings and weekends.

We slept in the living room until we were done with the bedrooms. We discovered that the house had some sparse furniture. The living room even had a huge faded Oriental rug with holes in it that looked decent after we washed it in the back yard. It is true that at one point, it gave us quite a fright, but more about that later. We threw out the box springs and had to replace the mattresses, naturally. They were crawling with tiny live creatures. Fortunately, we were supplied with almost new ones, mattresses that is, by one of the refugee relief agencies.

The cleanup process was rough and seemed interminable, but we were fueled by the determination to create a good home for our child and that made all the difficulties not only acceptable, but fun. We sang, we joked, we bantered until we were completely exhausted and collapsed at the end of the day.

One cold and rainy autumn evening, after finally managing to clean out the soot and ash and other messes from the fireplace in the living room, we lit a fire for the first time. We had a homestead now

—it was a grand occasion. We got a bottle of semi-decent red wine to celebrate. The lights shone dimly, but the fire was burning bright. The howling wind was drowned out by our chatter and songs. Both Robi and Bandi were gifted singers favoring Hungarian folk songs and Grand Opera. Mostly Bel Canto. We sang and danced, happy and exhausted and grateful for our good fortune. That's when the ghost turned up. The Oriental rug began to undulate and an eerie noise permeated the room. At first I thought I was imagining things in the dim light of the solitary bulb and the flickering shadows generated by the fire.

"Look!" I screamed, and the singing came to a screeching halt.

"Look at the floor!" I pointed to the far end of the room where the rug had begun to rise several inches, then subside very, very slowly. The men saw it too. The same phenomenon repeated itself in several other parts of the room. It was like ocean waves rising. For a few seconds, there was absolute silence, except for the wind howling outside. Then the men rose in unison to investigate, as men will. Especially engineers. None of us believed in ghosts, really. Not even in good old England. The odds that we were cleaning up a haunted house were just a bit too outlandish. So we dispersed, checking out every bit of the house and basement. We opened doors to look outside and Robi went down to the basement to look for pranksters. None were to be found. The rain stopped and the wind subsided. So did the carpet in the living room. We decided to go to bed.

The next day was a rare sunny Sunday and we reviewed the facts in the sober morning light. Was it the wine that made us imagine the carpet taking on a life of its own? That was unlikely. We had all seen and heard exactly the same things. The undulating carpet, the eerie, creepy sounds. When we decided to inspect the site of the previous night's revelries and hasty retreat, all we saw were abandoned plastic cups stained with red wine, half-eaten crackers, pieces of leftover cheese, and some odd crumbs of unidentifiable origin. The Oriental carpet was behaving now, lying still and prim, if faded, in the middle of the living room, looking quite unremarkable illuminated by the morning sun.

Robi started rolling it up. It was a big rug, so Bandi and I had to help.

"Why are we doing this?" I wanted to know.

Robi pointed to the emerging floorboards. They were uneven, with big gaps between them as they had settled over the years.

"Shoddy construction," Bandi said. "So what?"

"Well," said Robi "I went downstairs this morning and discovered that the basement door was blown half open by the storm last night. We did not see it in the dark. The wind came through the loose floorboards and kept on raising and dropping the thin rug. That's what we saw last night. We were not drunk, and there were no ghosts," he added smugly.

On the whole we were happy with this explanation. A sensible, engineering explanation. The light of reason vanquished the irrational once again. Still, part of me was reluctant to let go of the ghosts; they were so much more intriguing!

More intriguing than cooking, for instance. We had a kitchen now and no excuse whatsoever for not cooking. Never mind that I had no idea how. Following the success of our housecleaning we decided to celebrate and give a party. We invited Bandi and a few Hungarian friends. Everybody was talking about steaks being special and festive. We decided to make a go of it. The guys went out to get wine and cheese and crackers and I was to cook the beef, potatoes, and veggies. Well, I had never seen, eaten, or prepared steaks. In Hungary, beef was not particularly prized. It was tough and had the reputation of needing to be cooked as long as humanly possible to become edible. So that's what I did. Unfortunately, the longer the meat cooked, the tougher it got. So I cooked it some more. By the time the guys got home and the party time was not too far away, I had a pan full of inedible charred and shrunken bits of expensive steak. It smelled good, though. I used fresh herbs and good Hungarian paprika. Nevertheless, it ended up in the garbage. Even the neighbor's dog turned up his nose at it.

Pretty soon we had a lot more to worry about than ghosts and inedible steak. A polio epidemic was spreading in Europe and in the U.S. Young children were at the highest risk. The disease was often lethal. Those who did not die ended up paralyzed and in iron lungs. We saw terrible pictures in the papers. We did not have television. Dr. Salk had developed his vaccine in the U.S. in April 1955, a little more than a year before. As it was in the early stages of production, it was scarce and not available overseas, except in the most developed countries. Needless to say, Hungary was not one of them. My parents wrote about outbreaks around Lake Balaton, though not yet in Siofok. They thought it was just a matter of time until it arrived in their town. The disease evidently often clustered around and spread through contaminated water. Soon news of children and young adults crippled by or dying of polio in and around Siofok and elsewhere in the country reached us regularly. We panicked at first, then sprang into action to obtain the polio vaccine. We were ready to move heaven and earth through whatever means we could discover or imagine to succeed. We explored connections that we—or our parents or our friends, or their friends' friends—had in England or abroad, wrote letters to government and research organizations, and generally made a nuisance of ourselves until we were able to secure the necessary inoculation against polio and get it to my parents. It was a time of great anxiety and anguish. I am still amazed and grateful for all the help and support we got from everyone, and to Dr. Salk for developing this amazing vaccine, which led to the blessing of our baby being spared debilitating and deathly polio. We were grateful that she was thriving, developing into a lively, beautiful child of almost a year-and-a-half. My parents managed to smuggle out frequent photos providing plentiful evidence of this. We could not hear her laugh, but we could see her smile! We could not hold or cuddle her, but could see her snuggle up to my mother looking happy. It was not enough, but it kept us going. For now.

I loved to go shopping for her. We could not afford Mark and Spencer's, but the Army Navy Store was more affordable and the quality was solid. It was a huge department store at the time on Victoria Street, just south of St. James Park. It sold everything from a bar of soap to wedding dresses. Usually I bought necessities for Andrea and my parents that were not available in Hungary in those times of scarcity, such as high-quality baby food, dietary supplements, and ointments that did not make her break out in a rash, since she had very sensitive skin as did I. We sent well-made baby clothes, diapers, and other necessities, and toys of course. Coffee, tea and chocolate were luxuries for my parents that also allowed them to provide "welcome gifts" to people in the position to help with the unceasing efforts to get Andrea out of the country to join us. In any case, chocolate was regarded as a necessity in my family. It still is. At that time Cadbury chocolates were revered and coveted all over my native land. My favorites were Caramellos and the fruit and nut bars.

One day as I passed a small display shelf, my eyes were caught by a kangaroo. Now I am not a particular fan of kangaroos, but this one was simply adorable. She was off-white and graceful, with a tiny upturned nose made of some very lightweight soft and pliable rubbery substance. Her cheeks were pleasantly flushed as she smiled at her tiny offspring peering out of her pouch. She was a beautiful, happy, jolly little mummy kangaroo. She fit snuggly in my palm, and she was irresistible. I bought her. Robi thought it was one of my more impulsive purchases.

"Andrea does have plenty of toys; she does not need a rubber kangaroo," he pronounced. As it turned out, she did. As soon as it arrived in Siofok and she plucked it out of the package, she fell in love with it, or so I am told. It became her favorite toy. She would not let it go. She ate and slept and played with it. She talked to it. She learned how to say "kangaroo." She called it "Itsy Bitsy Kangaroo" in Hungarian. When she arrived in England several months later she was clutching it in her tiny hands. For many years after, before falling asleep, she would confide to the kangaroo all the important events of the day: who had made her cry, and who had made her happy. For many years, we listened regularly, if surreptitiously, outside her door, to find out what was really bothering her. This continued until she was nearly nine. Even after that, Itsy Bitsy Kangaroo occupied a prominent place among her prized possessions in spite of its many body cracks, faded cheeks and chewed off nose. I consider it one of the very best purchases I ever made.

My mother wrote every week, sometimes more than once. All the news that was fit to print, or at least all the news they hoped would not be censored. Generally about Andrea's latest antics and accomplishments. The first time she stood up, the first steps she took, the first words she said. Things she enjoyed or laughed at, what she liked to eat at the moment. We would hear about Father's latest health problems, his professional accomplishments, about relatives, and mutual friends. Important family events were described in detail as was the weather. Current events were avoided as was anything else that could be remotely considered political. Even so, the letters were heavily censored. Thick black lines blocked out much of the text. We could only guess what in my mother's chatty narratives could possibly have aroused suspicion of divulging state secrets! We knew that she could not write overtly about either the status or the details of progress concerning attempts to get our daughter out of Hungary to join us in England.

In spite of all this, it became increasingly clear, through coded language and metaphors, that D-day was approaching. News like "the canary fleeing the cage," or "the lost dog found again" suggested to us that Andrea's release from Hungary was coming closer every day. Naturally, this improvised code and hyperbole meant that we could never be quite sure that we understood properly what the message was exactly. We did our best and hoped it would be enough. We also thanked our good fortune several times a day that we finally lived in a free country where we did not have to prevaricate or fear the censor.

We set up a nursery in the house. We painted the walls a crisp, cheery white. We got pictures from the flea market, a lamp and a crib from the Refugee Agency. We invested in a second-hand dresser, a major investment. Got diapers from the Red Cross. Magdi donated some old baby blankets and a pram. We were ready! Or so we thought, until it became clear that Andrea was not coming alone!

It took us an excruciating ten months before we were able to arrange our Andrea's release from Hungary, and then only by stealth. Sometimes corruption has its advantages! Our parents were able to arrange a bribe through their connections and Andrea received permission to leave Hungary with her "mother!" You heard it right, her mother! Mami, my mother-in-law, who was well into her fifties by then, was listed as her mother on their passport.

Andrea was too young to be assigned to the care of a flight attendant. Even if it were possible, as we originally thought, the arrangements to allow her to leave Hungary called for her to travel with her mother on the same passport. Yes, her MOTHER! The ultimate absurdity of the absurd and corrupt bureaucracy then reigning in Hungary. Never mind that her birth mother was no longer in Hungary and could not return without being arrested and imprisoned for leaving the country illegally, as an enemy of the Regime. We needed to find a mother who was old enough and harmless enough to obtain a passport. So Mami, Robi's mother, volunteered to become a "mother" once again. Through rather obscure and complicated local and long-distance maneuvers involving money, barter, and bribery, she was able to obtain a passport and visa to leave the country for England with Andrea listed as her daughter. She was fifty-six at the time: neat, well put-together, but not a year younger looking. Her "daughter" was 18 months old. If anybody found this odd, no one mentioned it, although Mami later recalled a few tense moments at the Ferihegy Airport in Budapest (now Liszt Ferenc Airport) as border and customs agents examined her exit permits. It did not help that Andrea, rather verbal by that time, kept addressing her loudly and frequently as "Nagymama" or "grandma" in Hungarian. Fortunately, nobody seemed to pay attention to the chattering of a toddler.

It was thus that we became very busy getting another bedroom cleared out and ready in the house. Mr. Y of Aldershot was as good as his word…Both Andrea and Mami received English visas and permanent resident status promptly.

20. Andrea: Arrivals and Departures

 Done of the great mysteries of memory is its unevenness, its capricious nature. Why do I remember clearly and in great detail
trivial or insignificant things—such as cleaning up the house, or ru-
ining the steak—but only fragments or nothing at all of the extraordinary life-changing event: my daughter's arrival in England? An
event we had focused all our energies to bring about for ten months.
An event that would return to me the most precious thing in my life.
An event that finally promised to heal the wound and guilt of separation and complete my identity as an individual, a wife, a daughter,
and a mother. Yes, I am aware that most of us have the tendency to

My parents in Slofok

repress, even block, the memory of traumatic events, and that we prefer to remember mostly moments of joy and deliverance. Andrea's arrival was surely one of those moments, yet I remember very little of it.

I cannot describe the place where I first saw her at Heathrow. I have no idea what she wore, except that she carried Itsy Bitsy Kangaroo and kept pretty close to Mami. All I wanted to do was to embrace her, hug her, never let her go! But she did not know me. She had been eight months old when I last saw her; now she was a smart, active, verbal eighteen-month-old. I was a virtual stranger to her. I knew instinctively that I must not frighten or overwhelm her. I greeted her in Hungarian. I told her I was her mummy, and I loved her and missed her terribly. I gave her some chocolate and gifts. I don't remember what, but she loved them. I told her how beautiful her shining bright blue eyes were, that I loved hearing her voice, especially when she giggled, that I thought she was the cutest, smartest child ever. I can't recall what Robi said, but I suspect he did useful things like hugging his mother and taking care of the luggage. We both thanked Mami for bringing Andrea. Soon, but not soon enough, Andrea allowed me to hold her, to hug her, to feel her warmth, to stroke her soft wispy honey-colored hair, to comfort her. But she did not know me, and in many ways, I did not know her. There was a ten-month gap in our experiencing each other, an eternity for a young child, an eternity for me.

Perhaps I don't remember more because behind the joy of beholding my child was a vast river of unacknowledged pain of the last ten months—the fear that never left me, the fear of never seeing her again, the recognition that even though she was here now, I was a stranger to her. None of this was a complete surprise. For ten months I had been imagining her arrival in detail every time I missed her, which was every day. I prepared myself for possible, in fact probable, rejection ahead of time, and I had a plan, a strategy to regain her love, trust, and affection all over again. I knew I needed to spend as much time with her as possible, which meant finding a way to work at home.

I quit my full-time job at London Transport and, with Robi's help, set up a small, very small, business of knitting custom-designed garments on a then state-of-the-art knitting machine the refugee organization provided through a program to support small business ventures. They provided an exclusive line of high-fashion patterns for sweaters, cardigans, skirts, and shawls. They also provided outlets for the end products, if I remember correctly. The patterns were highly sophisticated and I wasn't exactly gifted in arts and crafts, to put it mildly. Fortunately, I always welcomed the challenge of learning new skills, especially since it promised the opportunity for a flexible schedule, the gift of caring for my baby and structuring work around her needs.

Both of these tasks turned out to be more of a challenge than I ever imagined. Learning again how to be a mom turned out to be tricky, time-consuming, and occasionally a source of frustration, but a perpetual delight. I learned to see the world again through my little girl's eyes. She delighted in sunshine and chasing the shadows of the clouds or her own shadow. She loved the chilly English rain, jumping into puddles, getting herself wet all over, resisting going home but laughing all the way. She would not miss any opportunity to chase birds, cats, squirrels, or any creature great or small that happened to cross our path.

Andrea seldom napped, since there were too many exciting things to do around the house. She did not even want to take time out for eating, for fear of missing any action! I had to think up amusing things to do with food to get her to eat. Little pieces of toast or fruit would take off in complicated flight patterns only to land in her mouth to be swallowed. Other pieces of edibles would appear to start an argument with each other or compete to reach her mouth first and make her strong! Andrea never got to be chubby, not then, not ever. Most of all, she liked to cuddle and be cuddled, at least briefly so as not to interrupt her predilection for perpetual motion and activity. No, she was not hyperactive, just a normal, precocious, energetic, inquisitive eighteen-month-old impatient to claim the world as her home. She was an absolute delight and profoundly exhausting to be around for anyone who was not a very young healthy person. Luckily, I was both young, healthy and highly energetic. Equally fortunately, Mami was more than happy to let me spend most of Andrea's waking time with her.

The knitting machine was harder to master and certainly a lot less fun. It was a formidable contraption. Big, heavy, and at least four to five feet long. We set it on a largish table so it would be out of reach for Andrea, or so we thought. It took Robi the better part of a day to figure out how it worked. After that, we chose a pattern for an elegant men's cardigan. We invested in a very expensive soft wool yarn, the color of pine trees. We ended up buying much more than needed because the pattern had instructions only for hand knitting, and we did not have a clue how using the machine would change that. Robi proceeded to program the knitting machine to recreate the pattern and hopefully create the hoped-for results. He did this by hand and it was a very complicated and tedious process. I could never have done it myself. You had to be an engineer or something. Remember, this was in 1957, and the age of automation had not yet progressed beyond the industrial scale.

Now I was ready to start work. Sort of. I had to learn how

to thread the wool and maintain the right tension to produce even stitches. I operated the machine by sliding a big square level from one end to the other for each row of stitches. It was pretty hard and tedious work requiring a lot of muscle strength and concentration. It was easy to make mistakes, which meant unraveling what I had already done. The cardigan had to be produced in four or five pieces. Mami assembled the finished product. She was an expert seamstress. It looked pretty good. It had raglan sleeves, a shawl collar, and light brown leather buttons with thin golden decorations. It was warm and cozy and truly a family effort. We decided to keep it as a prototype.

Alas, it soon became evident that the knitting machine was not a very cost-effective way to make a living. It was too labor intensive and it was hard to get enough money for the end product to produce a profit above the investment in high-quality wool and necessary accessories. So I found a part-time job in a nearby deli. It was winter and the meats and sausages had to be kept cold. It was freezing in the store. I learned to slice ham and cheese and salami razor-thin, and bologna, roast beef and sausages just so, and to estimate correctly how much I needed to cut of each to produce half-a-pound or a pound, to minimize waste. The store alternated between being very busy and very quiet according to some mysterious and unpredictable rhythm. Some of it made sense as it corresponded with lunch times or late afternoons when people were getting home from work. But even within these limits, customers tended to arrive in bunches, like seashells washed out by the surf, only to recede every fifteen to thirty minutes when a lull set in.

They were friendly and patient for the most part, putting up with my inexperience and heavy accent. I tried my best and smiled a lot. I was genuinely interested getting to know my customers. I did get tired, though, of the tedium of answering the omnipresent question,

"Where are you from, sweetie?" Eventually I made a game of it and let them guess. Everybody had three tries. Very few actually guessed the answer. Why, most of them had little notion that Hungary even existed. This was Wimbledon Park after all!

Still, it was hard work, being on your feet for four to six hours at a time in the cold store. I came to appreciate the difficulties involved in being an efficient salesperson. The upside was that we had plenty of fresh cold cuts and frankfurters, as the store gave us the leftover food to take home. The job paid reasonably well and I had a flexible schedule, so I could spend time with Andrea.

Happily, she very soon started calling me Anyu, or Anyuci, an affectionate diminutive of "Mummy" in Hungarian, when she was happy or wanted something special. I considered this a major break-through. There were others. We established a morning and bedtime routine. I would wake her in the morning and cuddle a bit and pre-pare breakfast. We would go for a walk in town or to a playground. Mami sometimes would come with us, but often was just as happy to stay home and rest or prepare lunch. She would also babysit when I had to work in the afternoon. We all had supper together when Robi came home, although Andrea would be fed earlier when he had to work late. After another walk or playtime, Robi and I would give her a bath and read bedtime stories before tucking her in for the night. It all happened more easily than expected. Her adaptability was amazing. She had been uprooted from her surroundings, lost the only caretakers she ever consciously remembered, my mother and father, and still she remained affectionate, trusting, and cuddly.

Andrea was inquisitive, chatty, and adventurous. When we went for a walk, it was hard to keep up with her, taking off in what seemed like every direction at the same time. She reminded me of a tiny humming bird hovering perpetually and at incredible speed, searching eagerly for experience, the honey of existence, wherever she could find it. She began to pick up English words almost immediately and was tirelessly active. She lived by simple rules illustrated by the following recurring dialogues:

"Honey, you have been running around for hours. You look tired," I said.

"No, I am NOT tired, I don't want to go in, please!"

Or I would ask, "Are you hungry? Let's go in and eat something. It's way past lunch time."

"No, I am not hungry at all! Please let's stay a little longer, pretty please…"

Finally, "It is bedtime, child, we need to slow down and get ready for bed."

"No, no, no, I am not sleepy, I am not tired, I need to finish building this castle," or pick up sticks, or a book, or whatever she happened to be busy with at the moment.

"But you can hardly keep your little eyes open!"

This would be followed by more denials and lengthy negotiations, often including bribery, such as milk, cookies and lengthy bedtime stories, until the issue got resolved. Naturally, as time passed, we were able to establish rules for a working routine. Nevertheless, Andrea seldom deviated from the simple rules she established early in childhood. She was never tired, never hungry, and never sleepy. Nowadays, more than 60 years later, she will sometimes admit to being hungry and occasionally sleepy.

We settled into a new kind of routine. I spent all my available time with Andrea, and Mami babysat when necessary. Andrea and I did the shopping, taking public transportation, and Mami came with us to familiarize herself with our neighborhood when she felt bored or adventurous, which was not very often. She kept busy around the house. She insisted on doing the cooking and Robi and I were in charge of washing up, though more often than not he used the time to be with his mother. I did not mind; I was perfectly content being with my daughter for the time being. I was also very aware of the sacrifices Mami had made by bringing Andrea to us. She had left behind her mother, her sisters, her friends, and the only country she ever knew for a foreign land where she did not understand either the language or the mores and customs. I understood that her need to be with her adult married son was every bit as strong as my need to be with my infant daughter. I understood and respected this, but soon began to dream of a day, sometime in the future, when Robi, Andrea, and I would have a place all to ourselves like a "normal" family. We would live close to Mami and involve her in our lives, but stay in separate households. I knew this wish was impractical, premature, and quite possibly unfair. I felt unkind as well as unreasonable when the thought surfaced. It was something I needed to work on.

The problem was that Mami and I had very little in common outside our bonds with Robi and Andrea. In retrospect, almost nothing. We did not speak the same language, although we both spoke Hungarian. Our interests and skills were nearly incompatible with hardly any overlap. Mami was sensitive, but lacked entirely any sense of humor. She had three sisters and had learned the skills to compete for equal treatment. I didn't. Both Robi and I were conflict averse and did our best to avoid her displeasure. It seemed OK, even sensible, in the short run, but was bound to create some problems later on.

On weekends we continued to explore London, but this time with Andrea and often with Mami in tow. It was delightful to watch their wide-eyed wonder at the architectural beauty of Westminster Abbey, Buckingham Palace and the grim atmosphere of the Tower.

Mami also enjoyed with deep wonder the richness and amazing variety of shops and department stores, and the hustle and bustle of Piccadilly Circus and Oxford Street. Andrea mostly chased the omnipresent pigeons. She was in seventh heaven in Trafalgar Square. It was hard to keep up with her as she darted back and forth, dodging the crowd, her tiny form disappearing in an instant if we relaxed our vigilance. In retrospect, she was incredibly fast and agile with seemingly unending energy. She still is.

Admonishing her to hold hands was a losing proposition when she was determined to explore on her own. In the end, we had to purchase a little harness for her, the end of which was attached to my wrist. It was baby blue tooled leather with little bears embellished on it. I called it a leash. I don't think this qualified as child abuse, because she did not mind and it allowed us to keep track of her without discouraging her independence. By the way, she would not stay in a stroller until she was completely exhausted, which was almost never. Her absolute favorites were the parks spread profusely all over the city. We loved all of them, St. James Park most of all because of the swans. She never tired of watching the swans.

Regents Park was also one of our go-to places and still is. We would go to the Zoo when we felt affluent. Mami wasn't exactly a zoo person, and she would stay home to relax or do some sewing for Andrea. She would get remaindered materials cheaply on our shopping expeditions and kept on making rather chic outfits for her granddaughter until she got very old and arthritic many decades later. Refugee or not, my daughter qualified as one of the best-dressed toddlers in London.

Magdi sometimes joined us with little John, but not very often. It was hard and expensive for her to travel to London, and the same was even more true for us to visit Brighton. So we mostly hung out with our friends, mostly other Hungarian refugees. Life was never dull when we got together. We were a high-spirited bunch and probably quite obnoxious by British standards. No stiff upper lip or dignified and introverted interactions for us. Temperamentally, we were closer to the cockneys than to the "educated classes." We had a lot of fun.

One day when our friends Eva and Pali showed up for a trip to the Zoo, they proudly displayed the sandwiches they had made for us for lunch. None of us could afford to eat out much, especially when we were going to spend money in the Zoo. The sandwiches were awful. I mean inedible. Really! They consisted of thin, stale, tasteless white bread topped with spam and some relish of unknown and undetermined origin. We insisted, "We're not hungry. We had a big late breakfast, but thank you anyway," and avoided possibly lethal exposure. Our decision was later vindicated by a far wiser creature, a beautiful elderly elephant. We were in the Zoo's open-air elephant habitat, where several of these giant animals were hanging out. We were actually staring at each other, I mean the elephants and us. They seemed as curious about us as we were about them. They were also seemingly hungry, their trunks reaching across the barrier inquisitively. Eva, now in the possession of excess sandwiches, decided to share. We pointed out a clearly visible "do not feed the animals" sign, but she ignored it with a shrug. Her half-sandwich was gratefully picked up by the long, very mobile trunk attached to a huge pachyderm. She brought the thing close to her face and carefully examined it. She practically shook her head and made a face while she ejected the half-sandwich in a large impressive arc of disdain. I don't think we stopped laughing for the rest of the day.

Some of our other adventures were less amusing. Once, after we left a popular movie theater on Oxford Street, we were animatedly discussing the film when our attention drifted to the people ahead of us. I am afraid we started to make fun of them, like stupid teenagers. Something about the garish colors they wore, the way they walked, trying to guess what part of England they might have come from, I truly can't remember. We did this in Hungarian, absolutely certain in our belief that no one could possibly understand us. Yes, I know this was not only immature but very rude as well. I am not proud of it. We had a lot of growing up to do. Also, in Budapest at that time, it was mostly OK to make fun of each other, since nobody took it seriously, they simply reciprocated. It was a kind of game. Anyway, yes, you guessed it, they turned around and gave us hell. They had understood every word…they were fellow Hungarians.

We apologized and were truly chastened. I have never made fun of others since. At least I hope I haven't. We also realized that, tiny as the country was, Hungarians were literally everywhere. Everybody who could had escaped, both at the time and historically. As a result, an astonishingly disproportionate number of Hungarians achieved world recognition in a wide variety of fields, from theoretical physics to music, acting, sports, and politics, just to name a few. Here are some names that might be familiar: Edward Teller and Leo Szilard of the Manhattan Project, instrumental in developing the atom bomb. Dubious distinction at best, but one that ended WWII and changed the world. Albert Szentgyorgyi, Nobel Prize winner in Physiology and Medicine. Conductors George Szell, George Solti, and pianists Andre Watts and Andras Schiff were Hungarian, as was half of Hollywood at the time of our stay in England. George Cukor, Leslie Howard, Tony Curtis, Mitzi Gaynor and the Gabor Sisters, among many others. Joseph Pulitzer, the publisher who established the famous Pulitzer Prize, was Hungarian. The list goes on and on and I haven't even mentioned sports or politics or contemporary artists. I still remember a joke widely circulating among the English at the time:

"How do you recognize a Hungarian?"

"He or she is the one entering the revolving door behind you, but getting out ahead."

Naturally, we didn't think this was particularly funny. The truth is that immigrants, by necessity, are hard-working, flexible self-starters, prepared to overcome hardships. Add to this that they are often also well-educated, especially when fleeing political oppression, and you get a highly capable group of people both then and now. I was aware that Robi was ambitious, but he was definitely not pushy, just insistent on surviving and doing his very best, which was pretty special indeed. I had dreams of proving myself eventually as a writer and theater director, but I knew I lacked both the qualifications and the required linguistic skills at that stage of my life. Like most women at the time, my immediate aim was more practical and centered around supporting my husband's career and becoming the best mother I could be. I simply wanted to be worthy of all the love bestowed on me by my husband, my child, and my parents while enjoying the freedom to make my own choices and experience life to the fullest. I did not see any contradictions or apparent conflicts in these goals. They began to emerge much later, or so I thought for a long time. In retrospect, they must have been there from the beginning.

It did not take long after Andrea and Mami's arrival for Robi to spring into action in order to bring about his dream to leave behind the austere and conservative shores of England for the opportunities and glamor of America. America was, for him and for most of the world, a kind of promised land, a land of opportunities. I don't remember being aware of what was happening. Whenever Robi brought up the subject, I made it very clear that I did not want to leave. I loved England. I liked the culture, the people, the values, and the lifestyle, difficult as it was. I admired the determination, endurance, and courage of the Brits during the war. They had suffered the way we had suffered; they too had hidden from the German bombs and taken refuge in shelters. They too had fought for survival and seen their homes, their cities destroyed and loved ones mutilated or killed. We understood each other. The only family I had close to my generation was here. I grew to love Magdi, John, and mercurial Imre.

England was part of Europe, part of everything I knew. In contrast, I knew next to nothing about the U.S. except what I saw in movies, both Westerns and glamorous Hollywood productions. I thought the Westerns scary and the Hollywood productions enjoyable, silly, and unrealistic. I only knew that the country was west, had relatively little past, and was very, very far from England and even farther from my parents and uncles in Hungary. Apart from everything else, I did not think I had the strength to uproot myself again and start again from scratch. I did not want to go.

I did not worry much about this, because immigration to the U.S. was tightly controlled at the time with strict quotas that required many years of waiting. I was stunned when one day in October, Robi announced that he had a job offer from Kaiser Aluminum in Chicago which exempted us from the quota. He was ecstatic. He would be hired on as a structural engineer for sophisticated and innovative high-profile designs at a beginning salary far exceeding his present wages or any wages he could ever get in England in the foreseeable future. He was convinced that it was the best thing that could ever have happened to us. The best thing not only for him, but for all of us, for the whole family. There was no question in his mind that we had to go.

"How, when did all this happen?" I wanted to know.

"I tried to tell you, but you did not want to talk about it."

"I thought it was your pipe dream, that it would never happen. The waiting list for Hungarian immigrants is years long."

"Kaiser is arranging all that. The U.S. decided it needed engineers badly after the Russians announced launching Sputnik, the world's first satellite. A few days ago, they actually did it successfully. Remember, it was all over the news recently?" I did. "Anyway, now engineers and some scientists are exempt from the quota, as long as they have a job that sponsors them. We can get out of here in a couple of months!"

He looked at me expectantly, beaming and happy and proud and full of anticipation. I did not say anything. I did not want to rain on his parade. He was so happy. At twenty-eight, he had just glimpsed the Promised Land. Robi knew me well enough to sense my distress. He spent the next several days lobbying for moving to the States. He had irrefutable arguments that it was our best opportunity to realize our potential and provide our family with the best possible life. He was convinced that America was the land of opportunity and freedom. The country had been built by immigrants like us, fleeing religious persecution and later persecutions of every kind. He was going to be able to support all of us, and I would be able to go back to school. Perhaps not immediately, but very soon.

How could I have said no? It would have been unreasonable and churlish at the least, or so I thought at the time, and Mami was ready to go. She had no particular ties to England. She would have gone anywhere in the world as long as she'd be with her son and granddaughter. Most importantly, I knew that Robi was objectively right on every count. The odds were that both his career and the family would prosper in the U.S. in ways they never would in the U.K. I also knew that he was not fully aware, could not be fully aware, of the emotional toll on me. He did not understand how difficult and painful it was for me to leave England behind.

The next few months were a blur. Robi promptly resigned his job and made all the official arrangements with the help of his new employer. We filled out endless paperwork. Passports and visas were issued, travel arrangements made. Packing was not a problem; we had very few belongings. We were ready to leave. We said goodbye to Magdi and young John, making pledges of continued contact. We hugged, vowing to never lose sight of each other again. I cried, and they kept a stiff upper lip, like good Brits. Saying goodbye to Imre was both easier and more difficult. I felt close to him, but knew almost nothing about him. We were the same age, but with vastly different experiences and lifestyles. Imre had lost both of his parents early and left a highly exclusive, prestigious public school at age sixteen. He had been there on a scholarship awarded only to highly talented students. It was an ill-advised decision, as he now sees clearly, but he was impatient to support himself, to make a living. He had no practical qualifications for existing jobs. He had to re-invent himself with very little, basically nonexistent, guidance. Eventually he did just that, and very successfully. But all that was in the future. His story is quite extraordinary. Perhaps I'll get the chance to tell it some other time. In 1958, we parted with high hopes but very little idea about what the future would bring.

In early February, in Southampton, we boarded the beautiful new French ship *SS Liberté*. Its state-of-the-art splendor was a sign of things to come, according to Robi. I hoped he was right. My cousins came to say goodbye. By now I was caught up in the general excitement and ready for the Great Adventure. At the ripe age of twenty-three, I was bracing to start yet another life, in the greatest country in the Free World, the amazing and wondrous and bewildering United States of America.

Epilogue

In due time, after five difficult but exciting years and after a con-siderable number of adventures, we all became American citizens. My son Peter was born in the United States in 1961.

Robi's predictions proved to be correct. He had an outstanding career both in academia and as a uniquely creative architectural engineer/designer. His professional accomplishments are visible all over the United States.

I never regretted becoming an American. I was soon caught up in the excitement and idealism of the civil rights movement, fol-lowed by the optimism and expanding consciousness of the "Age of Aquarius," and the women's movement in the sixties and be-yond. All or most of it spearheaded by my adopted country.

Father and Mother (Apu and Anyu) continued their lives in Siofok, Hungary, until he became seriously ill and needed state-of-the-art treatment available only in Budapest. They stayed with Uncle Rezso in the same apartment we were relocated after we lost our home in 1944. Luckily, this time it was less crowded, and there was enough to eat. I visited him in 1963 with Peter, the grandson he never met. He died shortly after at age 70. Anyu, my Mother, was heartbroken and seemed lost without him. We were able to arrange for her to eventually join us in Michigan, which she did enthusias-tically. Sadly, she had only a very brief time to enjoy her new life as she died 2 years later of cancer at the age of 57.

My uncles Rezso and Zoli both lived contentedly to a ripe old age in Budapest.

Mami adjusted well to moving to America. She even went back to work as a seamstress for a while, enjoying her independence in addition to being part of her son and grandchildren's lives. She lived to be 86, much loved, and well taken care of by her beloved family.

Magdi, my older cousin died tragically young in 1967 when her son John was only 14 years old. After a rough start John grew up to become a brilliant, highly respected solicitor and master chess player. He has been happily married to beautiful, talented, "Earth Mother" Philippa for many decades. They have a tight-knit family of two highly accomplished children and three grandchildren.

Imre after many adventures and overcoming great odds, became a highly successful businessman. He is living the good life in a fashionable part of London with his lovely, accomplished wife Jenny. He enjoys visiting his son Ben and is surrounded by his extended family. Though Imre is not quite as active as he used to be, his intellectual curiosity and zest for life are undiminished. He is 84.

Our friend Bandi settled in England . He could never again resume his career as an opera singer but seemed content to become a beloved professor of music at a university in Northern England.

My childhood friend Agi also escaped Hungary in 1956 with her husband. They eventually settled in Rhode Island where they became gifted and successful physicians serving their community until their retirement. They were blessed with a loving family of two children and three grandchildren.

AFTERWORD

I am a Holocaust Survivor. This makes me rather ancient, yet my central core feels disconcertingly timeless. A big part of me is stuck in young girlhood with its impulsivity, cockiness, and insecurities. Maturity and impetuous youth seem to coexist in shifting patterns, not split, but not exactly integrated either!

Being a Holocaust Survivor is one of my identities, but not the most inclusive, nor the most important or most descriptive. Yet it has deeply influenced who I became and how I chose to live my life. I have learned that although our experiences shape us, we can and often do shape our experiences.

I was eleven when World War II ended. I spent most of my childhood in the midst of war. It is not altogether surprising that from an early age on I was preoccupied with the apparent crapshoot of staying alive. Being an only child did not discourage excessive contemplation. I often battled panic, anxiety, and dread conjured up by the idea of non-being. Paradoxically, now that I am in fact approaching the chronological limits of my life, that fear is receding in intensity, the occasional flare-ups fueled more by learned patterns than conviction.

For decades after WWII, most of us kept our silence, attempting to forget, rebuild, and heal, with getting on with our lives. We were eager to be ordinary, not to stay marked forever by the "yellow star" the Nazis made us wear. We desperately wanted to shed our own particular scarlet letter.

I am not quite sure when things started to change but at some point, it became the "duty" of my generation to "bear witness." The pressure to do that has increased as it became evident that we won't be around much longer.

I have never particularly wanted to "bear witness." I was an unwilling witness to begin with. I most definitely did not want to, or choose to grow up in the midst of death, chaos, brutality, and persecution. I have often been asked to speak about the Holocaust and at times I have done so, including very recently at the U.S. Holocaust Memorial Museum, but on the whole, I have been reluctant to publicly revisit the past.

So, why did I write about it now? Mostly because I promised you, my beloved grandchildren, and because I am running out of time to yell and scream and shout out the memories of an unimaginably absurd childhood and adolescence in the naïve and probably vain hope, that it might be a warning to others not to repeat the past…

Liz, you started me on this book when you said to me years ago, "You have got to tell Your Story, Grandmother! You owe it to us, to future generations, so that we can remember. You have to write about it, so that it won't happen again!"

I had and still have my doubts.

"You think that people can learn from the past? Have you seen any evidence whatsoever to suggest that? You have majored in history. Did you see anything changing? As far as I can tell, only the labels change, or alternate, depending on current political trends and geographic location. Hostilities between Irish Catholics and Protestants, Christians and Muslims, Indians and Pakistanis, Sunnis and Shiites, Turks and Kurds, Serbs and Croats are all around us. I might add that ant-Semitism is on the rise once again, a historical constant, it seems over the ages.

There is an old Tom Lehrer song "National Brotherhood Week" describing the process in an entertaining and distressingly accurate way. It should be taught in schools and sung in churches, mosques and synagogues in my humble opinion, because mass murder and persecution still are the name of the game in much of the world. Even in our beautiful, free country intolerance is currently on the rise... The lessons of the past are so easily forgotten. "

Fortunately my desperate moods never last long. I am basically an optimist. We have made great strides towards autonomy, religious freedom, and equal rights in many parts of the world. The Nazis have been defeated and the Soviet Union crumbled, but moral evolution, just like biological evolution, takes a very long time. I believe that your generation is capable of making a difference for the better. I believe that you have the will and ability to learn from the past! So I wrote this story that is also your story. Use it wisely.

Do not be daunted
by the enormity
of the world's grief.

Do justly, now

Walk humbly, now

You are not obligated
to complete the work,

neither are you free
to abandon it.

-Talmud

ACKNOWLEDGEMENTS

Thank you to my many friends and family members for your interest and support of this project.

This book has been inspired by my grandchildren, Elisabeth and Tom Heller and Ella, Rachel and Josef Darvas. It could not have been completed without the enthusiastic encouragement and ongoing support of my wonderful friends and family.

Thank you, Pearl Seidman, for believing in me, providing early readings and feedback and generally maintaining an active and loving interest in the progress of this memoir.

Thank you everyone in my Writing Group. Without the discipline and camaraderie you provided, I may have given up on this project long ago. Special thanks to Peter Pollak, Mark McAllister, Rissa Miller and Robin Peace for urging me on and providing expert advice and editorial comments throughout the writing process. You truly kept me going from the very beginnings of this project by constantly reminding me that this story needed to be told.

Thank you Agi Somlo, Pam Millen, Jenny Lake for reading the early version of the manuscript and providing thoughtful feedback, comments, and encouragement.

Thank you, Karen Arnold, for taking time to review this work. Your thoughtful comments and suggestions surely made it a better read.

Many thanks to Betsy Hudson and Barbara Chavez for selflessly volunteering to edit the manuscript in spite of your busy full-time work schedule.

Much appreciation to Gabrielle deMers, my talented assistant. Although you joined this effort relatively recently, your research skills and relentless precision in hunting down remaining hidden inconsistencies and errors proved to be invaluable.

Last, but not least, I need to express my gratitude to the United States Holocaust Museum for making their archives available for research and giving permission to use images from their archives. Special thanks to Keri Bannister, Program Coordinator for Survivor Affairs, and Caroline Waddell Koehler, Photo Archivist, for greatly facilitating access to the material. Thank you also to Diane Saltzman, Director, Office of Constituency Engagement, for your kindness and interest in this project.

These notes would not be complete without declaring my enthusiastic appreciation to my long-suffering publisher Eileen Haavik McIntire. Her infinite patience with my ignorance of the ins- and-outs of book publishing made this book ultimately possible.

It is said that it takes a whole village to bring up a child. That is equally true of this book.

If I did not mention all the members of my village, it is because it is impossible to do so. I am thinking of you all with gratitude.

If you enjoyed this book,
please put a review on
Amazon.com

Consider this book
for your book club.

CPSIA information can be obtained
at www.ICGtesting.com
Printed in the USA
FSHW020907120819
60950FS

9 780999 156544